The Maids *and* Deathwatch

Two Plays

Jean Genet
With an Introduction by
Jean-Paul Sartre
Translated by Bernard Frechtman

First published in English translation
in the USA in 1954 by Grove Press Inc., New York
Revised edition published in 1962
First published in Great Britain in 1989
by Faber and Faber Limited
3 Queen Square London WC1N 3AU
Reprinted 1991

Printed in Great Britain by
Cox & Wyman Ltd, Reading, Berkshire
All rights reserved

A CIP record for this book is available from
the British Library

ISBN 0 571 14856 5

CONTENTS

INTRODUCTION

by JEAN-PAUL SARTRE

"Epimenides says that Cretans are liars. But he is a Cretan. Therefore he lies. Therefore Cretans are not liars. Therefore, he speaks the truth. Therefore, Cretans are liars. Therefore, he lies, etc." This is the argument of Epimenides. It is the model of circular sophistry as bequeathed by ancient scepticism. Truth leads to the lie and vice-versa.

The mind that enters one of these vicious circles goes round and round, unable to stop. With practice, Jean Genet has managed to transmit to his thought an increasingly rapid circular movement. He has a vision of an infinitely rapid rotation which merges the poles of appearance and reality, just as, when a multi-colored disk is spun quickly enough, the colors of the rainbow interpenetrate and produce white. Genet constructs such whirligigs by the hundred. They become his favorite mode of thinking. He indulges knowingly in false reasoning.

The most extraordinary example of the whirligigs of being and appearance, of the imaginary and the real, is to be found in his play, *The Maids*. It is the element of fake, of sham, of artificiality, that attracts Genet in the theatre. He has turned dramatist because the falsehood of the stage is the most manifest and fascinating of all. Perhaps nowhere has he lied more brazenly than in *The Maids*.

Two maids both love and hate their mistress. They have denounced her lover to the police by means of anonymous letters. Upon learning that he is to be released for lack of proof, they realize that their betrayal will be discovered, and they try to murder Madame. They fail and want to kill themselves. Finally, one of them takes her life, and the other, left alone and drunk with glory, tries, by the pomp of her posturings and language, to be equal to the magnificent destiny that awaits her.

Let us indicate at once a first whirligig. Genet says in *Our Lady of the Flowers*: "If I were to have a play put on in which women had roles, I would demand that these roles be performed by adolescent boys, and I would bring this to the attention of the spectators by means of a placard which would remain nailed to the right or left of the sets during the entire performance." [1] One might be tempted to explain this demand by Genet's taste for young boys. Nevertheless, this is not the essential reason. The truth of the matter is that Genet wishes from the very start to *strike at the root of the apparent*. No doubt an actress can play Solange, but what might be called the "de-realizing" would not be radical, since there

[1] *The Maids* was actually performed by women, but this was a concession which Genet made to Louis Jouvet, who produced the play.

would be no need for her to play at being a woman. The softness of her flesh, the languid grace of her movements and the silvery tone of her·voice are natural endowments. They constitute the substance that she would mold as she saw fit, so as to give it the appearance of Solange. Genet wishes this feminine stuff itself to become an appearance, the result of a make-believe. It is not Solange who is to be a theatrical illusion, but rather *the woman Solange.*

In order to achieve this absolute state of artifice, the first thing to do is to eliminate nature. The roughness of a breaking voice, the dry hardness of male muscles and the bluish luster of a budding beard will make the de-feminized and spiritualized female appear as an invention of man, as a pale and wasting shadow which cannot sustain itself unaided, as the evanescent result of an extreme and momentary exertion, as the impossible dream of man in a world without women.

Thus, what appears behind the footlights is not so much a woman as Genet himself living out the impossibility of being a woman. We would see before us the effort, at times admirable and at times grotesque, of a youthful male body struggling against its own nature, and, lest the spectator be caught up in the game, he would be warned throughout—in defiance of all the laws of stage perspective—that the actors are trying to deceive him as to their sex. In short, the illusion is prevented from "taking" by a sustained contradiction between the effort of the actor, who measures his talent by his ability to deceive, and the warning of the placard. Thus, Genet *betrays* his actors. He unmasks them, and the performer, seeing his imposture exposed, finds himself in the position of a culprit who has been found out. Illusion, betrayal, failure; all the major categories that govern Genet's dreams are here present. In the same way, he betrays his characters in *Our Lady of the Flowers* and in *Funeral Rites* by warning the reader whenever the latter is about to yield to the illusion of the story: "Watch out. These are creatures of my imagination. They don't exist." The thing to be avoided above all is the spectator's being caught up in the game, like children at the cinema who scream, "Don't drink it, it's poison!" or like the naive public that waited at the stage-door for Frédéric Lemaître in order to beat him up.

To seek being through appearance would be to make *good use* of the latter. For Genet, theatrical procedure is demoniacal. Appearance, which is constantly on the point of passing itself off as reality, must constantly reveal its profound unreality. Everything must be so false that it sets our teeth on edge. But by virtue of being false, the woman acquires a poetic density. Shorn of its texture and purified, femininity becomes a heraldic sign, a cipher. As long as it was natural, the feminine blazon remained embedded in woman. Spiritualized, it becomes a category of the imagination, a device for generating reveries. Anything can be a woman: a flower, an animal, an inkwell.

In *The Child Criminal* Genet has given us the keys of what might be called his algebra of the imagination. He speaks of the director of a home for children who boasts of giving the children tin knives and who adds, "They can't kill anyone with that." Genet makes the following comment: "Was he unaware that by departing from its practical destination the object is transformed, that it becomes a symbol? Its very form sometimes changes. We say that it becomes stylized. It then acts secretly in children's souls. It does more serious damage. Hidden at night in a straw mattress or concealed in the lining of the jacket or, rather, of the trousers—not for greater convenience, but in order to be close to the organ it symbolizes—it is the very sign of the murder that the child will not actually commit but which will feed his reverie and, I hope, will direct it toward the most criminal manifestation. What good does it do to take it away from him? The child will only choose some more harmless-looking object as a sign of murder, and if this also is taken from him, he will guard within him preciously the sharper image of the weapon." As the material grows poorer—steel knife, tin knife, hazel-twig—as the distance increases between itself and what it signifies, the symbolic nature of the sign is heightened. The reveries are directed, fed and organized. His maids are fake women, "women of no gynaeceum", who make men dream not of possessing *a* woman but of being lit up by a woman-sun, queen of a feminine heaven, and finally of being themselves the matter for the heraldic symbol of femininity. Genet is trying to present to us femininity without woman.

Such is the initial direction of his de-realization: a falsification of femininity. But the shock boomerangs and the performance affects the actor himself. The young murderer,

Our Lady of the Flowers, dresses up as a woman one day just for the fun of it. "Our Lady, in his pale blue faille dress, edged with white Valenciennes lace, was more than himself. He was himself and his complement." We know that Genet values above all the labor of de-realization. The thing that attracts him in Our Lady of the Flowers is the spectacle of a man being worked upon by femininity: "Our Lady raised his bare arm and—it's astounding—this murderer made the very same gesture, though a trifle more brutal, that Emilienne d'Alençon would certainly have made to rumple her chignon." This hybrid creature, of the race of centaurs and sirens, begins as a male only to go up in smoke as female fireworks. In order to express his superiority both to young men and to all women, Genet invents a wonderful sign: "The chauffeur opened the door . . . Gorgui, because of his position in the group, ought to have stepped in first, but he moved aside, leaving the opening free for Our Lady. Bear in mind that never does a pimp efface himself before a woman, still less before a fairy . . . Gorgui must have placed him quite high." The appearance of the imaginary upsets social conventions. Gorgui the Pimp spontaneously adopts bourgeois courtesy. He effaces himself before a glamourous young male who de-realizes himself into a young lady whose grace is heightened by the glamor of the murderer. The grace of women is usually despised by roughnecks because it signifies weakness and submission. But here it shimmers at the surface of the great and dark force of killers. Hence, they must bow before it. Crime becomes the secret horror of grace; grace becomes the secret softness of crime. Our Lady is the vestal of a blood-thirsty goddess, a great cruel Mother of a homosexual matri-archy.

Thus far we have seen nothing we did not already know. All this is still the reciprocal de-realization of matter by form and of form by matter. But now the first whirligig is set going. Genet's poetic themes are, as we know, profoundly homosexual. We know that neither women nor the psychology of women interests him. And if he has chosen to show us maids and their mistress and feminine hatreds, it is only because the necessities of public performance oblige him to disguise his thought. The proof of this is that his second play, *Deathwatch*, the characters of which are all men, deals with exactly the same subject as *The Maids*.

There is the same hierarchy: in one case, Monsieur, in the other, Snowball; the intermediate divinity, Madame and Green Eyes; and the two youngsters who dream of murder but fail to commit it, who love and hate each other and each of whom is the other's bad smell, Solange and Claire, Maurice and Lefranc. In one case, the play ends with a suicide that the police will take for a murder; in the other, with a fake murder, that is, a real killing which rings false. Lefranc, who is a fake, is a real traitor; Maurice, however, who is too young to kill, is of the race of killers; thus, they too form "the eternal couple of the criminal and the saint", as do Divine and Our Lady. This is the same eternal couple that Solange and Claire want to form. And their ambiguous feel-ing for Madame is discreetly homosexual, as is that of Lefranc and Maurice for Green Eyes. Moreover, Genet himself has known the maids' hatred of Madame. He tells us in *Our Lady of the Flowers* that he himself was once a servant, and in *Funeral Rites* he tells us of another servant, the suffering mother who concealed beneath her skirts "the craftiest of hoodlums." Similarly, it has been said that "Proust's Albertine should be called Albert." The young actors in *The Maids* are boys playing at being women, but these women in turn are secretly boys. However, these imaginary boys who gleam behind the feminine appearances of Solange and Claire are not to be identified with the real adolescents who embody the characters. They too are dreams, since in the other play they are called Maurice and Lefranc. They are, if you like, on the vanishing-line of the appearances, giving them their appearance of depth. But the spectators dimly sense the homosexual drift of the plot, and when the actor raises his bare arm and reveals too much muscle, when he adjusts his bun and makes a gesture "a trifle more brutal" than that of Emilienne d'Alençon, the spectator does not know whether this inordinate muscularity and too evident brutality represent a rebellion of reality or whether they transcend this story about women and symbolize homosexuality. Are the dry and angular gesture and the brusque gait merely the awkwardness of a young male hampered by a woman's dress, or are they not Maurice, who has taken possession of Solange? Are they a return to Being or are they the quintessence of the imaginary? Being changes at this point into appearance and appearance into being. But it may be objected that the homo-

14

sexual drama is the *truth* of this ancillary fiction. Well and good. But it is an appearance which becomes the truth of another appearance. And then, in another sense, these fake women were the truth of the adolescent boys who embodied them, for Genet, like all homosexuals, is able to discern a secret femininity in the most male of men. As in psychodramas, his actors play what they are. They resemble, feature for feature, the real hoodlum who played the fake-prince-who-is-a-real-hoodlum and who, through the mediation of the prince, was de-realized into himself. But if these fake women are the disguise of imaginary men, the young actors are swallowed up by a new absence. As they interpret their own drama, they are the unconscious pawns in a game of chess which Genet is playing against himself.

But we are still at only the first degree of de-realization. These fake women who are fake men, these women-men who are men-women, this perpetual challenging of masculinity by a symbolic femininity and of the latter by the secret femininity which is the truth of all masculinity, are only the faked groundwork. Upon this evanescent foundation there appear individual forms: Solange and Claire. We shall see that they too are faked.

The play has four characters, one of whom does not appear, namely, Monsieur, the *man*. Monsieur is Harcamone of *Miracle of the Rose;* he is Snowball of *Deathwatch.* Pilorge is he who *is never there*. His absence represents the eternal abstraction of the handsome Pimps, their indifference. In this bourgeois atmosphere he is the only one who is ennobled by prison. To be sure, he is slanderously accused of a crime which he has not committed, but we know that for Genet guilt comes to the offender from without. It is a collective image, a taboo that settles upon him. Behind this homosexual *Arlésienne* whom everyone talks about and nobody sees is Madame, an ambiguous figure, a mediation, a girl-fairy in relation to Monsieur and a man-fairy in relation to the two maids. To Monsieur she is a faithful dog. Genet ascribes to her his old dream of following a convict to the penal-colony. "I wanted to be," he tells us, "the young prostitute who accompanies her lover to Siberia." And Madame says: "I don't think he's guilty either, but if he were, I'd become his accomplice. I'd follow him to Devil's Island, to Siberia." But something warns us—perhaps her volubility or the wild gaiety of her despair—that she is a fraud. Does she love Monsieur? Probably she does. But to what point? There is no way of telling. At all events, she has found, like Ernestine in *Our Lady of the Flowers*, the finest role of her life. It will be noted that Green Eyes, a symmetrical character who is also an intermediary and a "daimon," though he has committed an honest-to-goodness murder, plays, in his state of exaltation, at being a murderer. In Genet's plays every character must play the role of a character who plays a role. In relation to the two maids, Madame represents pitiless indifference. Not that she despises or mistreats them; she is *kind*. She embodies social Good and Good Conscience, and the servants' ambivalent feelings about her express Genet's feelings about Good. She feels sorry for them: she gives them dresses; she loves them, but with an icy love, "like her bidet." In like manner, wealthy, cultivated and happy men have, from time to time, "felt sorry" for Genet, have tried to oblige him. Too late. He has blamed them for loving him for the love of Good, *in spite of* his badness and not for it. Only an evil individual could love another evil individual for the love of Evil. But evil-doers do not love.

As a woman in relationship to Monsieur, Madame has only *relative* being. As the maids' mistress, she retains an absolute being. But the maids are relative to everything and everyone; their being is defined by its absolute relativity. They are *others*. Domestics are pure emanations of their masters and, like criminals, belong to the order of the Other, to the order of Evil. They *love* Madame. This means, in Genet's language, that both of them would like to *become* Madame, in other words, to be integrated into the social order instead of being outcasts. They *hate* Madame. Translate: Genet detests the Society that rejects him and he wishes to annihilate it. These specters are born of the dream of a master; murky to themselves, their feelings come to them from outside. They are born in the sleeping imagination of Madame or Monsieur. Low, hypocritical, disagreeable and mean because their employers dream them that way, they belong to the "pale and motley race that flowers in the minds of decent people." When he presents them before the footlights, Genet merely mirrors the fantasies of the right-minded women in the audience. Every evening five hundred Madames can sing out, "Yes, that's what maids are like," without realizing that they have created them, the way Southerners create Negroes. The only rebellion of these flat creatures is that they rebel in turn: they dream within a dream; these dream dwellers, pure reflections of a sleeping consciousness, use the little reality which this consciousness has given them to imagine that they are becoming the Master who imagines them. They flounder about at the intersection of two nightmares and form the "twilight guard" of bourgeois families. They are disturbing only in that they are dreams who dream of swallowing up their dreamer.

Thus, the maids, as Genet conceives them, are *already* fake. Pure products of artifice, their minds are inside out, and they are always other than themselves. That there are two of them is a stroke of genius. Two, exactly the number needed to set up a whirligig. To be sure, Genet did not invent these criminal sisters out of whole cloth. The reader has probably recognized Claire and Solange; they are the Papin sisters. But we already know that Genet has distilled the anecdote, that he has retained only its quintessence and presents it to us as a "cipher." The *maids* are the mysterious cipher of the pure imagination and also of Genet himself. There are two of them because Genet is double: himself and the other. Thus, each of the two maids has no other function than to be the other, to be—for the other—herself-as-other. Whereas the unity of the mind is constantly haunted by a phantom duality, the dyad of the maids is, on the contrary, haunted by a phantom of unity. Each sees in the other only herself at a distance from herself. Each bears witness to the other of the impossibility of *being* herself, and, as Querelle says[1]: "their double statue is reflected in each of their halves." The mainspring of this new whirligig is the perfect interchangeability of Solange and Claire, which makes Solange always appear to be elsewhere, *on* Claire when we look at Solange, and *on* Solange when we look at Claire. To be sure, this interchangeability does not exclude certain differences. Solange seems harder; perhaps "she tries to dominate" Claire; perhaps Genet has chosen her to embody the glamorous appearance and the secret cowardice of the criminal; perhaps he has elected the gentle and perfidious Claire to symbolize the hidden heroism of the Saint. In actual fact, Solange's attempts at crime fail: she manages to kill neither Madame nor her own sister. Claire also botches a murder, but, pushing their play-acting to its extreme consequences, she takes her own life. The girl-fairy has more real courage than the tough one. This means that the fake courage of Solange finds its truth in the secret courage of Claire, that the fake pusillanimity of Claire finds its truth in the profound cowardice of Solange.

But Genet does not linger over these familiar themes, which he develops abundantly elsewhere. Solange and Claire are much less differentiated than Maurice and Lefranc; their dissimilarities are dreams which ill conceal a fundamental identity. Both of them are characterized by the imaginary splendor of their projects and the radical failure of their undertakings. In reality, Genet has set before us *a single object*, though a profoundly faked one, neither one nor two,

[1] In Genet's novel *Querelle of Brest* (Translator's note).

one when we want to see two, two when we want to see one: the ancillary couple as a pure criss-cross of appearances. And the bond that unites these two reflections is itself a faked relationship. Do the sisters love each other, do they hate each other? They hate each other with love, like all of Genet's characters. Each finds in the other her "bad smell" and one of them proclaims that "filth doesn't love filth." But at the same time, each inwardly clings to the other by a kind of carnal promiscuity which gives to their caresses the tepid pleasure of masturbation. But where is the truth of the ancillary couple? When we see Solange and Claire in the presence of Madame, they do not seem real. Fake sumbission, fake tenderness, fake respect, fake gratitude. Their entire behavior is a lie. We are led to believe that his falsifying comes from their fake relationships with their mistress. When they resume their joint solitude, they put on their true faces again. But when they are alone, they play. Claire plays at being Madame and Solange at being Claire. And we await, despite ourselves, the return of Madame which will cause their masks to fall and which will restore them to their true situation as servants.

Thus, their truth is always elsewhere; in the presence of the Masters, the truth of a domestic is to be a fake domestic and to mask the *man* he is under a guise of servility; but, in their absence, the *man* does not manifest himself either, for the truth of the domestic in solitude is to play at being master. The fact is that when the Master is away on a trip, the valets smoke his cigars, wear his clothes and ape his manners. How could it be otherwise, since the Master convinces the servant that there is no other way to become a man than to be a master. A whirligig of appearances: a valet is sometimes a man who plays at being a servant and sometimes a servant who plays at being a man; in other words, a man who dreams with horror that he is becoming a sub-man or a sub-man who dreams with hatred that he is becoming a man.

Thus, each of the two maids plays, in turn, at being Madame. When the curtain rises, Claire is standing in front of the dressing-table of her mistress. She is experimenting with Madame's gestures and language. For Genet, this is an actual incantation. We shall see later on that, by imitating the gestures of his superior, the domestic treacherously draws him into himself and becomes saturated with him. There is nothing surprising in this, since Madame herself is a fake Madame who plays at distinction and at her passion for Monsieur and who dreams of drawing into herself the soul of a whore who follows her pimp to jail.

Similarly, Genet could, without difficulty, *make himself* Stilitano[1] because Stilitano himself played at being Stilitano. Madame is no more true in Claire than in Madame herself; Madame is a gesture.

Solange helps her sister put on one of her mistress' dresses, and Claire, playing her role in a state of exaltation, taut and strained, as is Genet himself, insults Solange, as she does every evening, until the latter, driven to extremities, as she

[1] In *The Thief's Journal* (Translator's note).

is every evening, slaps her. This is, of course, a ceremony, a sacred game which is repeated with the stereotyped monotony of schizophrenic dreams. In short, Genet, whose reveries are themselves often dry and ceremonious and who repeats them day after day until their charm is exhausted, introduces the spectator into the very privacy of his inner life. He allows himself to be overheard in a spell of incantation; he betrays himself; he gives himself away; he hides nothing of the monotony and childishness which spoil his secret festivities and of which he is perfectly aware. And he even invites us to see what he himself will never see because he is unable to get outside himself: the inside and outside, the *reality* (if there is one) and its disguise. As for the role itself, we recognize quite easily Genet's favorite themes: to begin with, the maids *want*, to the point of despair and horror, the servile condition that is imposed upon them; in like manner, Genet wants to be the bastard, the outcast that society has made of him. And this cruel game provides the rigorous demonstration of what we suggested a while ago: one can not want to be what one is in the imaginary; in order to live their wretchedness to the point of *passion*, down to the dregs, they must make themselves the cause of it. Thus, Solange plays the role of servant. But she would be sticking too close to reality if she remained Solange; there would be no way of deciding whether she takes upon herself her menial condition or whether she *really*, and out of habit, performs her servile tasks. In order to change herself into a maid by her own will, Solange *plays at being* Solange. She can not *want to be* Solange the servant, because she *is* Solange. She therefore wants to be an imaginary Claire so as to acquire one of the chief characteristics of this Claire, which is to be a servant. A phantom Claire dresses an imaginary Madame. Here a small local whirl is set up: an actor plays the role of a servant who is playing the role of a servant. The falsest of appearances joins the truest being, for to play at being a maid is the truth of the actor and the phantasy of Solange. The result is —and this does not fail to delight Genet—that in order "to be true" the actor must *play false*. The fact is that Solange, who is not a professional actress, plays her role of maid badly. Thus, the nearer the actor draws to his reality as actor, the further he withdraws from it. Fake jewels, sham pearls, Genet's deceptive loves: an actor plays at being an actor, a maid plays at being a maid; their truth is their lie and their lie is their truth. The same may be said of the actor playing the role of Claire-playing-Madame; Genet confirms it in his stage directions: "Her gestures and tone are exaggeratedly tragic."

The reason for this is that the ceremony has still another meaning: it is a Black Mass. What is played every evening is the murder of Madame, a murder always being interrupted, always uncompleted. It is a case of committing *the worst*: Madame is benevolent, "Madame is kind"; they will kill their benefactress, precisely because she has been Good to them. The act will be imaginary, since Evil is the imagination. But *even in the imaginary* it is faked in advance. The maids know that they will not have time enough to get to the crime.

> "SOLANGE: The same thing happens every time. And it's all your fault, you're never ready. I can't finish you off.
> CLAIRE: We waste too much time with the preliminaries."

Thus, the playing of the sacrilege conceals a failure in behavior. It is imaginary to the second degree: Claire and Solange do not even play the fictitious murder; they pretend to play it. They are thereby merely imitating their creator. As I have pointed out elsewhere, Genet prefers imaginary murder to real murder because in the former the will to evil, though remaining entire, pushes the love of nothingness to a point where it reduces itself to impotence. In the last analysis, Solange and Claire are fully satisfied with this *appearance* of crime; what they like about it more than anything else is the taste of nothingness with which it leaves them. But they both pretend, by means of a further lie, that they are disappointed at not having gone through with the thing to the very end. And besides, what would there have been "at the very end"? The true murder of the fake Madame? The fake murder of Claire? Perhaps they don't even know themselves.

The fact remains that in this phantom play-acting, which,

even as play acting, never concludes,[1] the great role this
evening is reserved for Claire: it is for her to personify
Madame and so to exasperate Solange that she commits a
crime. But Solange personifies Claire. Whence, a new dis-
integration: the relationships of the fake Madame with the
fake Claire have a triple, a quadruple basis. In the first place,
Claire makes herself be Madame *because she loves her*; for
Genet, to love means to want to be. As Madame, she blossoms
out; she escapes from herself. But in addition, she makes
herself be Madame *because she hates her*: resentment de-
realizes; Madame is merely a passive phantom who is slapped
on Claire's cheeks. Besides, the interpretation of Claire is
forced; she is not aiming at showing Madame as she is, but
at making her hateful. Madame, the sweet and kind Madame,
insults her maids, humiliates them, exasperates them. And
we do not know whether this distorted caricature tends to
reveal the mistress in her true light, to expose the truth of
that indifferent good-nature which may be concealing a pitiless cruelty, or whether it already wreaks an imaginary vengeance by metamorphosizing Madame, by the incantation of
the gesture, into a harpy. As psychoanalysis has revealed to
us, one of the motives of acts of self-punishment is to force
the judge to punish unjustly and thereby to burden him with
a guilt which discredits him and makes him unworthy of
judging. By means of her interpretation of Madame's role,

[1] Genet is an old hand at these unfinished ceremonies. He confides to us in
Miracle of the Rose that he used to caress Bulkaen in thought but would
abandon him even before attaining erection.

Claire transforms her into an unjust judge and rids herself of her. But at the same time, in the guise of Madame, she insults and humiliates Solange, whom she hates, Solange, her bad smell: "Avoid pawing me. You smell like an animal. You've brought those odors from some foul attic where the lackies visit us at night." But Solange is sheltered: she is playing the role of Claire. First, as we have seen, because it is easier for her as the fake Claire to assume her menial condition; then, because Claire can be Madame only if she seems Madame in her own eyes. Solange's becoming Claire represents the astounding effort of a reflective consciousness turning back on itself and wanting to perceive itself as it appears to others. This attempt is doomed to failure; either the reflective consciousness is real and its object melts into the imaginary (Genet can *see himself* as a thief only poetically), or else the object remains real and it is the reflection that slips into the imaginary (Eric, in *Funeral Rites*, imagines seeing himself with the eyes of the executioner). Solange's play-acting belongs to this second category; it is Claire taking upon herself a reflective view in the imaginary. Claire's audience is the phantom of herself-as-other. It is thus *herself* whom she humiliates; it is to *herself* that she says: "Keep your hands off mine! I can't stand your touching me." Solange, Madame, the intermediate appearances, all vanish. Claire stands alone facing her mirror, in the desert. Thus, the love-hatred she feels for Madame conceals her feeling for Solange and finally her feeling about herself. And each of these feelings has an imaginary side; her hatred of Madame takes on a double aspect; in so far as Claire is the source of it, she de-realizes herself and exhausts herself in her caricatural interpretation of this character; but, on the other hand, she passes into Solange, who, as fake Claire, directs upon the fake Madame, on behalf of her sister, a fictive hatred. As for Claire's hatred of Solange, it is completely covered and disguised by the play-acting: it is not, to be sure, fictive, but it finds within reach only fictive instruments and modes of expression; in order to hate Solange, Claire has no other resource but to make herself Madame-hating-Claire. Finally, Claire's hatred of herself makes it necessary that at least one of the two terms of this affective relationship be imaginary: in order to hate and to love, there must be two; hence, Claire can hate only a phantom of herself embodied by Solange. But we again fall upon a whirligig: for *at the same time* the feelings are true; it is true that Claire hates Madame, true that she hates Solange and that, through the mediation of Solange, she tries to hate herself. Once again the fake is true and the true can be expressed only by means of the fake. And when Claire calls Solange "you clod", when Solange, *in ecstasy*, cries, "Madame's being carried away!" *who* is insulting *whom*? And *who* feels the insult with that masochistic pleasure? Inversely, *who* tempts *whom* to commit murder? And *who* slaps *whom*? This slap is a sacred rite which represents the rape of Genet by the Male. But this whirligig of appearances has made us so dizzy that we do not know whether it is Claire who slaps Madame, Claire who slaps Claire, Solange who slaps Claire or Solange who slaps

27

Solange.[1] It may be objected that the fact remains that the true Solange has performed a real act and that the true Claire has felt true pain. So they have. But the same holds for this slap as for Genet's thefts. As I have pointed out elsewhere, though these thefts were *really* committed, they were lived in the imaginary. This slap is therefore a poetic act. It melts into a gesture; the very pain that it causes is lived imaginarily. At the same time, moreover, it is slurred over, for this true slap which is felt imaginarily is a fake slap that an actor pretends to give another actor.

This extraordinary faking, this mad jumble of appearances, this superimposing of whirligigs which keep sending us back and forth from the true to the fake and from the fake to the true, is an infernal machine whose mechanism Genet is careful not to reveal to us at the beginning. When the curtain goes up, we see an impatient and nervous young lady who is rebuking her maid. From time to time an unusual word or an inappropriate gesture casts a disturbing light upon this familiar scene. But suddenly an alarm-clock goes off: "The two actresses, in a stage of agitation, run together. They huddle and listen." Claire, in a changed voice, mutters: "Let's hurry! Madame'll be back." She starts to unfasten her dress. "It's so close this evening;" they are "exhausted and sad;" in order to put their short black skirts on again they need some of that "greatness of soul" that Divine displayed when she put her bridge back into her mouth. However, the spectator, in a dazzling flash, sees

[1] For Solange hates herself in Claire as Claire in Solange.

28

through the heart of the darkness to this astounding mechanism of appearances: everything was fake; the familiar scene was a diabolical imitation of everyday life. The entire scene was prepared in order to impose this deception upon us.

The high value of appearance is due, in Genet's eyes, to the fact that, like Evil, of which it is the pure embodiment, it eats at and does away with itself. Cases of volatilization are rare in ordinary life; the plate breaks and the pieces remain. But appearance offers us a certain being. It gives it to us, it hands it over to us, and, if we put out our arm, this being is suddenly reabsorbed. The victim of the three-card trick has not lost sight of the ace of hearts; he *knows* that it is the first card of the third pack; he points to it; the performer turns it up: it's the ace of spades. He then feels a strange and brutal disappointment in his flesh. For a moment he thinks that he has an intuition of nothingness. Yes, the nothing becomes an apparition, non-being a richness which fills him; the absence of the ace of hearts is much more virulent, much more immediate, than the presence of the ace of spades. The following instant his perception has regained its fullness, but the instant remains mysterious. The nothingness has disappeared; it allowed itself to be glimpsed and then vanished.

But since non-being *is not*, how can it *no longer be*? It is this perverse intuition that Genet prefers to all else: it makes the *nothing* shimmer at the surface of *all*. Where is being? Can it be that something *is*? If the ace of hearts has vanished, why should not the ace of spades disappear as well? And

29

what is non-being, if it can suddenly fill me with its emptiness? In *The Maids*, the ambiguous instant of deception, when superimposed illusions collapse like a house of cards, rightly deserves the name of pure instant of the Lie. For when the Saharan mirage vanishes, it reveals true stones. But when the deceptive appearances in the play are dispelled, they reveal in their place *other appearances* (the fake Madame becomes Claire again, the fake maid, the fake woman; the fake Claire becomes Solange again, the fake servant). At this moment the spectator has first the demoniacal intuition of nothingness, that is, being is revealed to be nothing, but, as appearance is usually effaced in the presence of being, the illusions which vanish leave him with the illusion that *it is being* which replaces them. Suddenly the pantomime of a young male who pretends to be a woman *seems to him to be the truth.* It is as if he suddenly understood that the only true thing is play-acting, that the only real women are men, and so on. Being has been revealed as non-being and thereupon non-being becomes being. This moment in which the lights flicker, when the volatile unity of the being of non-being and the non-being of being is achieved in semi-darkness, this perfect and perverse instant, makes us realize from within the mental attitude of Genet when he dreams: it is the moment of evil. For in order to be sure of never making *good use* of appearance, Genet wants his fancies, at two or three stages of de-realization, to reveal themselves in their nothingness. In this pyramid of fantasies, the ultimate appearance de-realizes all the others. Thus, the youngster who plays the role of Claire is de-realized into a young man so that the latter may be de-realized into a mistress. But, as I have shown, an appearance borrows its being from being: thus, "Claire" borrows her being from the boy who interprets her. But the "fake Madame" is supported in being by *Claire*, who does not exist. And since she thus derives her being from a fantasy, the being of this appearance is only an appearance of being. Whereupon Genet considers himself satisfied; on the one hand, he has achieved pure appearance, the one whose very being is appearance, that is, the one which appears to be appearance through and through, to borrow nothing from being and finally to produce itself, which, as we know, is one of the two contradictory demands of Evil; but, on the other hand, this pyramid of appearances masks the being which supports them all (the true movement, the true words uttered by the young actor in the play, the movement and words which, in actual life, help Genet dream), and as, nevertheless, they *are* in some way, it seems that each borrows its being from the one that immediately precedes it. Thus, as being fades into appearance at all degrees, it seems that the real is something melting, that it is reabsorbed when touched. In these patient fakings, appearance is revealed at the same time as pure nothingness and as cause of itself. And being, without ceasing to set itself up as absolute reality, becomes evanescent. Translated into the language of Evil: Good is only an illusion; Evil is a Nothingness which arises upon the ruins of Good.

THE MAIDS

A Play in One Act

The Maids was originally published in French as *Les Bonnes* in *L'Arbalète,* No. 12 (Lyons: 1947).

Les Bonnes was first performed at the Théâtre Athénée in Paris on April 17, 1947. It was produced and directed by Louis Jouvet, and the décor was designed by Christian Bérard.

Solange	Monique Mélinand
Claire	Yvette Etiévant
Madame	Yolande Laffont

THE CHARACTERS

SOLANGE } Two housemaids, sisters, thirty to thirty-five
CLAIRE } years old. Solange is the elder.

MADAME   Their mistress. She is about twenty-five.

THE MAIDS

Madame's bedroom. Louis-Quinze furniture. Lace. Rear, a window opening on the front of the house opposite. Right, a bed. Left, a door and a dressing table. Flowers in profusion. The time is evening.

[CLAIRE, *wearing a slip, is standing with her back to the dressing table. Her gestures—arm extended—and tone are exaggeratedly tragic.*]

CLAIRE:

Those gloves! Those eternal gloves! I've told you time and again to leave them in the kitchen. You probably hope to seduce the milkman with them. No, no, don't lie; that won't get you anywhere! Hang them over the sink. When *will* you understand that this room is not to be sullied. Everything, yes, everything that comes out of the kitchen is spit!

So stop it! [*During this speech,* SOLANGE *has been playing with a pair of rubber gloves and observing her gloved hands, which are alternately spread fanwise and folded in the form of a bouquet.*] Make yourself quite at home. Preen like a peacock. And above all, don't hurry, we've plenty of time. Go!

[SOLANGE'S *posture changes and she leaves humbly, holding the rubber gloves with her fingertips.* CLAIRE *sits down at the dressing table. She sniffs at the flowers, runs her hand over the toilet articles, brushes her hair, pats her face.*] Get my dress ready. Quick! Time presses. Are you there? [*She turns round.*] Claire! Claire!

[SOLANGE *enters.*]

SOLANGE:

I beg Madame's pardon, I was preparing her tea. [*She pronounces it "tay."*]

CLAIRE:

Lay out my things. The white spangled dress. The fan. The emeralds.

SOLANGE:

Very well, Madame. All Madame's jewels?

CLAIRE:

Put them out and I shall choose. And, of course, my patent-leather slippers. The ones you've had your eye on for years. [SOLANGE *takes a few jewel boxes from the closet, opens them, and lays them out on the bed.*] For your wedding, no doubt. Admit he seduced you! Just look at you! How big you are! Admit it! [SOLANGE *squats on the rug, spits on the patent-leather slippers, and polishes them.*] I've told you, Claire, with*out* spit. Let it sleep in you, my child, let it stagnate. Ah! Ah! [*She giggles nervously.*] May the lost wayfarer drown in it. Ah! Ah! You *are* hideous. Lean forward and look at yourself in my shoes. Do you think I find it pleasant to know that my foot is shrouded by the veils of your saliva? By the mists of your swamps?

SOLANGE [*on her knees, and very humble*]:
I wish Madame to be lovely.

CLAIRE:
I shall be. [*She primps in front of the mirror.*] You hate me, don't you? You crush me with your attentions and your humbleness; you smother me with gladioli and mimosa. [*She stands up and, lowering her tone*] There are too many flowers. The room is needlessly cluttered. It's *impossible.* [*She looks at herself again in the glass.*] I shall be lovely. Lovelier than you'll ever be. With a face and body like that, you'll never seduce Mario. [*Dropping the tragic tone*] A ridiculous young milkman despises us, and if we're going to have a kid by him—

SOLANGE:
Oh! I've never—

CLAIRE [*resuming*]:
Be quiet, you fool. My dress!

SOLANGE [*she looks in the closet, pushing aside a few dresses*]:

The red dress. Madame will wear the red dress.

CLAIRE:

I said the white dress, the one with spangles.

SOLANGE [*firmly*]:

I'm sorry. Madame will wear the scarlet velvet dress this evening.

CLAIRE [*naively*]:

Ah? Why?

SOLANGE [*coldly*]:

It's impossible to forget Madame's bosom under the velvet folds. And the jet brooch, when Madame was sighing and telling Monsieur of my devotion! Your widowhood really requires that you be entirely in black.

CLAIRE:

Eh?

SOLANGE:

Need I say more? A word to the wise—

CLAIRE:

Ah! So you want to talk. . . . Very well. Threaten me. Insult your mistress, Solange. You want to talk about Monsieur's misfortunes, don't you? Fool. It was hardly the moment to allude to him, but I can turn this matter to fine account! You're smiling? Do you doubt it?

SOLANGE:

The time is not yet ripe to unearth—

CLAIRE:
What a word! My infamy? My infamy! To unearth!

SOLANGE:
Madame!

CLAIRE:
Am I to be at your mercy for having denounced Monsieur to the police, for having sold him? And yet I'd have done even worse, or better. You think I haven't suffered? Claire, I forced my hand to pen the letter—without mistakes in spelling or syntax, without crossing anything out—the letter that sent my lover to prison. And you, instead of standing by me, you mock me. You force your colors on me! You speak of widowhood! He isn't dead. Claire, Monsieur will be led from prison to prison, perhaps even to Devil's Island, where I, his mistress, mad with grief, shall follow him. I shall be in the convoy. I shall share his glory. You speak of widowhood and deny me the white gown—the mourning of queens. You're unaware of that, Claire—

SOLANGE [coldly]:
Madame will wear the red dress.

CLAIRE [simply]:
Quite. [Severely] Hand me the dress. Oh! I'm so alone and friendless. I can see in your eyes that you loathe me. You don't care what happens to me.

SOLANGE:
I'll follow you everywhere. I love you.

CLAIRE:

No doubt. As one loves a mistress. You love and respect me. And you're hoping for a legacy, a codicil in your favor—

SOLANGE:

I'd do all in my power—

CLAIRE [*ironically*]:

I know. You'd go through fire for me. [SOLANGE *helps* CLAIRE *put on her dress.*] Fasten it. Don't pull so hard. Don't try to bind me. [SOLANGE *kneels at* CLAIRE's *feet and arranges the folds of the dress.*] Avoid pawing me. You smell like an animal. You've brought those odors from some foul attic, where the lackeys visit us at night. The maid's room! The garret! [*Graciously*] Claire, if I speak of the smell of garrets, it is for memory's sake. And of the twin beds where two sisters fall asleep, dreaming of one another. There, [*she points to a spot in the room*] there, the two iron beds with the night table between them. There, [*she points to a spot opposite*] the pinewood dresser with the little altar to the Holy Virgin! That's right, isn't it?

SOLANGE:

We're so unhappy. I could cry! If you go on—

CLAIRE:

It *is* right, isn't it! Let's skip the business of your prayers and kneeling. I won't even mention the paper flowers. . . . [*She laughs.*] Paper flowers! And the branch of holy box-wood! [*She points to the flowers in the room.*] Just look at

these flowers open in my honor! Claire, am I not a lovelier
Virgin?

SOLANGE [*as if in adoration*]:
Be quiet—

CLAIRE:
And there, [*she points to a very high spot at the window*]
that notorious skylight from which a half-naked milkman
jumps to your bed!

SOLANGE:
Madame is forgetting herself, Madame—

CLAIRE:
And what about your hands? Don't *you* forget your hands.
How often have I [*she hesitates*] murmured: they befoul
the sink.

SOLANGE:
The fall!

CLAIRE:
Eh?

SOLANGE [*arranging the dress on* CLAIRE'S *hips*]:
The fall of your dress. I'm arranging your fall from grace.

CLAIRE:
Get away, you bungler! [*She kicks* SOLANGE *in the temple
with her Louis-Quinze heel.* SOLANGE, *who is kneeling,
staggers and draws back.*]

SOLANGE:
Oh! Me a burglar?

CLAIRE:

I said bungler; and if you must whimper, do it in your garret. Here, in my bedroom, I will have only noble tears. A time will come when the hem of my gown will be studded with them, but those will be precious tears. Arrange my train, you clod.

SOLANGE [*in ecstasy*]:

Madame's being carried away!

CLAIRE:

By the devil! He's carrying me away in his fragrant arms. He's lifting me up, I leave the ground, I'm off. . . . [*She stamps with her heel.*] And I stay behind. Get my necklace! But hurry, we won't have time. If the gown's too long, make a hem with some safety pins. [SOLANGE *gets up and goes to take the necklace from a jewel case, but* CLAIRE *rushes ahead of her and seizes the jewels. Her fingers graze those of* SOLANGE, *and she recoils in horror.*] Keep your hands off mine! I can't stand your touching me. Hurry up!

SOLANGE:

There's no need to overdo it. Your eyes are ablaze.

CLAIRE [*shocked astonishment*]:

What's that you said?

SOLANGE:

Limits, boundaries, Madame. Frontiers are not conventions but laws. Here, my lands; there, your shore—

CLAIRE:

What language, my dear. Claire, do you mean that I've already crossed the seas? Are you offering me the dreary exile of your imagination? You're taking revenge, aren't you? You feel the time coming when, no longer a maid—

SOLANGE:

You see straight through me. You divine my thoughts.

CLAIRE [*increasingly carried away*]:

—the time coming when, no longer a maid, you become vengeance itself, but, Claire, don't forget—Claire, are you listening?—don't forget, it was the maid who hatched schemes of vengeance, and I—Claire, you're not listening.

SOLANGE [*absent-mindedly*]:

I'm listening.

CLAIRE:

And I contain within me both vengeance and the maid and give them a chance for life, a chance for salvation. Claire, it's a burden, it's terribly painful to be a mistress, to contain all the springs of hatred, to be the dunghill on which you grow. You want to see me naked every day. I *am* beautiful, am I not? And the desperation of my love makes me even more so, but you have no idea what strength I need!

SOLANGE [*contemptuously*]:

Your lover!

CLAIRE:

My unhappy lover heightens my nobility. Yes. Yes, my child. All that you'll ever know is your own baseness.

SOLANGE:

That'll do! Now hurry! Are you ready?

CLAIRE:

Are you?

SOLANGE [*she steps back to the wardrobe*]:

I'm ready.—I'm tired of being an object of disgust. I
hate you, too. I despise you. I hate your scented bosom.
Your . . . *ivory* bosom! Your . . . *golden* thighs! Your . . .
amber feet! I hate you! [*She spits on the red dress.*]

CLAIRE [*aghast*]:

Oh! . . . Oh! . . . But. . . .

SOLANGE [*walking up to her*]:

Yes, my proud beauty. You think you can always do just as
you like. You think you can deprive me forever of the
beauty of the sky, that you can choose your perfumes and
powders, your nail-polish and silk and velvet and lace, and
deprive *me* of them? That you can steal the milkman from
me? Admit it! Admit about the milkman. His youth and
vigor excite you, don't they? Admit about the milkman.
For Solange says: to hell with you!

CLAIRE [*panic-stricken*]:

Claire! Claire!

SOLANGE:

Eh?

CLAIRE [*in a murmur*]:

Claire, Solange, Claire.

SOLANGE:

Ah! Yes, Claire, Claire says: to hell with you! Claire is here,
more dazzling than ever. Radiant! [*She slaps* CLAIRE.]

CLAIRE:

Oh! . . . Oh! Claire. . . . You. . . . Oh!

SOLANGE:

Madame thought she was protected by her barricade of
flowers, saved by some special destiny, by a sacrifice. But
she reckoned without a maid's rebellion. Behold her wrath,
Madame. She turns your pretty speeches to nought. She'll
cut the ground from under your fine adventure. Your Monsieur was just a cheap thief, and you—

CLAIRE:

I forbid you! Confound your impudence!

SOLANGE:

Twaddle! She forbids me! It's Madame who's confounded.
Her face is all convulsed. Would you like a mirror? Here.
[*She hands* CLAIRE *a mirror.*]

CLAIRE [*regarding herself with satisfaction*]:

I see the marks of a slap, but now I'm more beautiful than
ever!

SOLANGE:

Yes, a slap!

CLAIRE:

Danger is my halo, Claire; and you, you dwell in darkness. . . .

SOLANGE:

But the darkness is dangerous.—I know. I've heard all that
before. I can tell by your face what I'm supposed to answer.

So I'll finish it up. Now, here are the two maids, the faithful servants! They're standing in front of you. Despise them. Look more beautiful.—We no longer fear you. We're merged, enveloped in our fumes, in our revels, in our hatred of you. The mold is setting. We're taking shape, Madame. Don't laugh—ah! above all, don't laugh at my grandiloquence. . . .

CLAIRE:
Get out!

SOLANGE:
But only to be of further service to Madame! I'm going back to my kitchen, back to my gloves and the smell of my teeth. To my belching sink. You have your flowers, I my sink. I'm the maid. You, at least, you can't defile me. But! But! . . . [*she advances on* CLAIRE, *threateningly*.] But before I go back, I'm going to finish the job. [*Suddenly an alarm clock goes off.* SOLANGE *stops. The two actresses, in a state of agitation, run together. They huddle and listen.*] Already?

CLAIRE:
Let's hurry! Madame'll be back. [*She starts to unfasten her dress.*] Help me. It's over already. And you didn't get to the end.

SOLANGE [*helping her. In a sad tone of voice*]:
The same thing happens every time. And it's all your fault, you're never ready. I can't finish you off.

CLAIRE:

We waste too much time with the preliminaries. But we've still. . . .

SOLANGE [*as she helps* CLAIRE *out of her dress*]:

Watch at the window.

CLAIRE:

We've still got a little time left. I set the clock so we'd be able to put the things in order. [*She drops wearily into the armchair.*]

SOLANGE [*gently*]:

It's so close this evening. It's been close all day.

CLAIRE [*gently*]:

Yes.

SOLANGE:

Is that what's killing us, Claire?

CLAIRE:

Yes.

SOLANGE:

It's time now.

CLAIRE:

Yes. [*She gets up wearily.*] I'm going to make the tea.

SOLANGE:

Watch at the window.

CLAIRE:

There's time. [*She wipes her face.*]

SOLANGE:

Still looking at yourself . . . Claire, dear. . . .

CLAIRE:

Let me alone. I'm exhausted.

SOLANGE [*sternly*]:

Watch at the window. Thanks to you, the whole place is in a mess again. And I've got to clean Madame's gown. [*She stares at her sister.*] Well, what's the matter with you? You can be like me now. Be yourself again. Come on, Claire, be my sister again.

CLAIRE:

I'm finished. That light's killing me. Do you think the people opposite. . . .

SOLANGE:

Who cares! You don't expect us to . . . [*she hesitates*] organize things in the dark? Have a rest. Shut your eyes. Shut your eyes, Claire.

CLAIRE [*she puts on her short black dress*]:

Oh! When I say I'm exhausted, it's just a way of talking. Don't use it to pity me. Stop trying to dominate me.

SOLANGE:

I've never tried to dominate you. I only want you to rest. You'll help me more by resting.

CLAIRE:

I understand, don't explain.

SOLANGE:

Yes, I will explain. It was you who started it. When you

mentioned the milkman. You think I ████
were driving at? If Mario—

CLAIRE:

Oh!

SOLANGE:

If the milkman says indecent things to me, he does to you, too. But you loved mingling. . . .

CLAIRE [*shrugging her shoulders*]:

You'd better see whether everything's in order. Look, the key of the secretary was like this [*she arranges the key*] and, as Monsieur says—

SOLANGE [*violently*]:

You loved mingling your insults—

CLAIRE:

He's always finding the maids' hairs all over. the pinks and roses!

SOLANGE:

And things about our private life with—

CLAIRE:

With? With? With what? Say it! Go on, name it! The ceremony? Besides, we've no time to start a discussion now. She'll be back, back, back! But, Solange, this time we've got her. I envy you; I wish I could have seen the expression on her face when she heard about her lover's arrest. For once in my life, I did a good job. You've got to admit it. If it weren't for me, if it hadn't been for my anonymous letter, you'd have missed a pretty sight: the lover handuffed and Madame in tears. It's enough to kill her. This morning she could hardly stand up.

SOLANGE:

Fine. She can drop dead! And I'll inherit! Not to have to set foot again in that filthy garret, with those two idiots, that cook and that butler.

CLAIRE:

I really liked our garret.

SOLANGE:

Just to contradict me. Don't start getting sentimental about it. I loathe it and I see it as it really is, bare and mean. And shabby. But what of it! We're just scum!

CLAIRE:

Ah! No, don't start that again. Better watch at the window. I can't see a thing. It's too dark outside.

SOLANGE:

Let me talk. Let me get it out of my system. I liked the garret because it was plain and I didn't have to put on a show. No hangings to push aside, no rugs to shake, no furniture to caress—with my eyes or with a rag, no mirrors, no balcony. Nothing forced us to make pretty gestures. Don't worry, you'll be able to go on playing queen, playing at Marie Antoinette, strolling about the apartment at night.

CLAIRE:

You're mad! I've never strolled about the apartment.

SOLANGE [*ironically*]:

Oh, no. Mademoiselle has never gone strolling! Wrapped

in the curtains or the lace bedcover. Oh no! Looking at herself in the mirrors, strutting on the balcony at two in the morning, and greeting the populace which has turned out to parade beneath her windows. Never, oh no, never.

CLAIRE:

But, Solange—

SOLANGE:

It's too dark at night for spying on Madame, and you thought you were invisible on your balcony. What do you take me for? Don't try to tell me you walk in your sleep. At the stage we've reached you can admit it.

CLAIRE:

But, Solange, you're shouting. Please, please lower your voice. Madame may come in without making a sound. . . . [*She runs to the window and lifts the curtain.*]

SOLANGE:

All right, I've had my say. Let go of the curtains. Oh, I can't stand the way you lift them. Let go of them. It upsets me; that's how Monsieur did it when he was spying on the police, the morning he was arrested.

CLAIRE:

So you're scared now? The slightest gesture makes you feel like a murderer trying to slip away by the service stairway.

SOLANGE:

Go on, be sarcastic, work me up! Go on, be sarcastic! Nobody loves me! Nobody loves us!

CLAIRE:

She does, *she* loves us. She's kind. Madame is kind! Madame adores us.

SOLANGE:

She loves us the way she loves her armchair. Not even *that* much! Like her bidet, rather. Like her pink enamel toilet-seat. And we, can't love one another. Filth . . .

CLAIRE:

Ah! . . .

SOLANGE:

. . . doesn't love filth. D'you think I'm going to put up with it that I'm going to keep playing this game and then at night go back to my folding-cot? The game! Will we even be able to go on with it? And if I have to stop spitting on someone who calls me Claire, I'll simply choke! My spurt of saliva is my spray of diamonds!

CLAIRE [*she stands up and cries*]:

Speak more softly, please, please. Speak—speak of Madame's kindness.

SOLANGE:

Her kindness, is it? It's easy to be kind, and smiling, and sweet—ah! that sweetness of hers!—when you're beautiful and rich. But what if you're only a maid? The best you can do is to give yourself airs while you're doing the cleaning or washing up. You twirl a feather duster like a fan. You make fancy gestures with the dishcloth. Or like *you*, you treat yourself to historical parades in Madame's apartment.

CLAIRE:

Solange! You're starting again! What are you trying to do? We'll never calm down if you talk like that! I could say a thing or two about you.

SOLANGE:

You? You?

CLAIRE:

Yes, me. If I wanted to. Because, after all. . . .

SOLANGE:

All? After all? What are you insinuating? It was you who started talking about that man. Claire, I hate you.

CLAIRE:

Same to you and more! But if I wanted to provoke you, I wouldn't have to use the milkman as an excuse. I've got something better on you and you know it.

SOLANGE:

Who's going to get the better of who? Eh? Well, say something?

CLAIRE:

Go on, start it! You hit first. It's you who're backing out, Solange. You don't dare accuse me of the worst: my letters. Pages and pages of them. The garret was littered with them. I invented the most fantastic stories and you used them for your own purposes. You frittered away my frenzy. Yesterday, when you were Madame, I could see how delighted you were at the chance they gave you to stow away on the *Lamartiniere,* to flee France in the company of your lover—

SOLANGE:

Claire—

CLAIRE:

Your lover, to Devil's Island, to Guiana. You were delighted that my letters allowed you to be the prostitute kneeling at the feet of the thief. You were happy to sacrifice yourself, to bear the cross of the impenitent thief, to wipe his face, to stand by him, to take his place in the galleys so that he could rest. And you felt yourself growing. Your brow rose higher than mine, it rose above the palm trees.

SOLANGE:

But what about you, just before, when you were talking about following him. . . .

CLAIRE:

Right. I don't deny it. I took up where you left off. But with less violence than you. Even in the garret, amidst all the letters, you started swaying back and forth with the pitching of the boat.

SOLANGE:

You didn't see yourself—

CLAIRE:

I did. I'm more sensible than you. You're the one who concocted the story. Turn your head. Ha! If only you could see yourself, Solange. Your face is still lit up by the sun setting through the virgin forest! You're planning his es-

cape! [*She laughs nervously.*] You certainly do work yourself up! But don't let it worry you; it would be cruel to
disturb your blissful voyage. I hate you for other reasons,
and you know what they are.

SOLANGE [*lowering her voice*]:
I'm not afraid of you. I know you hate me and that you're
a sneak, but be careful now. I'm older than you.

CLAIRE:
So what?—Older! And stronger too? You're trying to put
me off by making me talk about that man. Hmph! You
think I haven't found you out? You tried to kill her.

SOLANGE:
Are you accusing me?

CLAIRE:
Don't deny it. I saw you.

[*A long silence.*]

And I was frightened. Frightened, Solange. Through her,
it was me you were aiming at. I'm the one who's in danger.
When we finish the ceremony, I'll protect my neck.

[*A long silence.* SOLANGE *shrugs her shoulders.*]

SOLANGE [*with decision*]:
Is that all? Yes, I did try. I wanted to free you. I couldn't
bear it any longer. It made me suffocate to see you suffocat-
ing, to see you turning red and green, rotting away in that
woman's bitter-sweetness. Blame me for it, you're right. I
loved you too much. Had I killed her, you'd have been the

first to denounce me. You'd have turned me over to the police, yes, you.

CLAIRE [*she seizes her by the wrists*]:
Solange. . . .

SOLANGE [*freeing herself*]:
What are *you* afraid of? It's *my* concern.

CLAIRE:
Solange, my little sister, she'll be back soon.

SOLANGE:
I didn't kill anyone. I was a coward, you realize. I did the best I could, but she turned over in her sleep. [*Rising exaltation*] She was breathing softly. She swelled out the sheets: it was Madame.

CLAIRE:
Stop it.

SOLANGE:
Now you want to stop me. You wanted to know, didn't you. Well, wait, I've got some more to tell you. You'll see what your sister's made of. What stuff she's made of. What a servant girl really is. I wanted to strangle her—

CLAIRE:
Let me alone. Think of what comes after.

SOLANGE:
Nothing comes after. I'm sick and tired of kneeling in pews. In church I'd have had the red velvet of abbesses or the stone of the penitents, but my bearing at least would have been noble. Look, just look at how she suffers. How she

suffers in beauty. Grief transfigures her, doesn't it? Beautifies her? When she learned that her lover was a thief, she stood up to the police. She exulted. Now she is forlorn and splendid, supported under each arm by two devoted servants whose hearts bleed to see her grief. Did you see it? Her grief sparkling with the glint of her jewels, with the satin of her gowns, in the glow of the chandelier! Claire, I wanted to make up for the poverty of my grief by the splendor of my crime. Afterward, I'd have set fire to the lot.

CLAIRE:

Solange, calm down. The fire might not have caught. You'd have been found out. You know what happens to incendiaries.

SOLANGE:

I know everything. I kept my eye and ear to the keyhole. No servant ever listened at doors as I did. I know everything. Incendiary! It's a splendid title.

CLAIRE:

Be quiet. I'm stifling. You're stifling me. [*She wants to open the window.*] Oh! Let's have some air!

SOLANGE:

Get away from the window. Open the anteroom and the kitchen doors. [CLAIRE *opens both doors.*] Go and see whether the water's boiling.

CLAIRE:

All alone?

SOLANGE:

Wait, all right, wait till she comes. She's bringing her stars, her tears, her smiles, her sighs. She'll corrupt us with her sweetness.

[*The telephone rings. The two sisters listen.*]

CLAIRE [*at the telephone*]:

Monsieur? It's Monsieur! . . . This is Claire, Monsieur. . . . [SOLANGE *wants to hear too, but* CLAIRE *pushes her away.*] Very well. I'll inform Madame. Madame will be overjoyed to hear that Monsieur is free. . . . Yes, Monsieur. . . . Very well. . . . Good-by, Monsieur. [*She wants to hang up, but her hand trembles, and she lays the receiver on the table.*]

SOLANGE:

Is he out?

CLAIRE:

The judge let him out on bail.

SOLANGE:

Well, you've done a fine job. My compliments. Your denunciations, your letters, it's working out beautifully. And if they recognize your handwriting, it'll be perfect.

CLAIRE:

Please, please, don't overwhelm me. Since you're so clever, you should have managed your business with Madame. But you were afraid. The bed was warm. The air thick with perfume. It was Madame! We've got to carry on with the same kind of life. With the same old game. But, you poor wretch! Even the game is dangerous. I'm sure we've left traces. We leave them every time. I see a host of traces I'll never be able to cover up. And she, she walks about in her tamed menagerie. She unravels the clues. She points to our traces with the tip of her pink toe. She discovers us, one by one. Madame jeers at us. And it's your fault. All's lost because you lacked strength.

SOLANGE:

I can still find whatever strength I need.

CLAIRE:

Where? Where? You've been outstripped by *me*. You don't live above the treetops. A milkman passing through your mind gets you all flustered.

SOLANGE:

It was because I couldn't see her face, Claire. Because I was so close to Madame, so close to her sleep. I lost my strength. In order to get at her throat, I'd have had to lift the sheet from her heaving bosom.

CLAIRE [*ironically*]:

And the sheets were warm. The night dark. That kind of thing has to be done in broad daylight. You're incapable of it. It's too terrible a deed. But *I* can manage it.

SOLANGE:

Claire!

CLAIRE:

Where you botched it, *I'll* succeed.

SOLANGE [*she runs a comb through her hair*]:

Claire, don't get carried away, don't be rash—

CLAIRE:

What makes you think I'm being rash? First of all, don't
mix your hairpins up with mine! You . . . . Oh! All right,
mix your muck with mine. Mix it! Mix your rags with my
tatters! Mix it all up. It'll stink of the maids. So Monsieur
won't have any trouble discovering us. And we'll die in a
flood of shame. [*Suddenly calm*] I'm capable of anything,
you know.

SOLANGE:

The sleeping pills.

CLAIRE:

Yes. Let's talk calmly. I'm strong. You tried to dominate
me. . . .

SOLANGE:

But, Claire—

CLAIRE [*calmly*]:

I beg your pardon, but I know what I'm saying. I've made
up my mind. I'm ready. I'm tired of it all. Tired of being
the spider, the umbrella-case, the shabby, godless nun,
without a family! I'm tired of having a stove for an altar.
I'm that disagreeable, sullen, smelly girl. To you, too.

SOLANGE:

Claire . . . we're both nervous. [*Anxiously*] Where's Madame? I can't stand it any more either. I can't stand our
being so alike, I can't stand my hands, my black stockings,
my hair. I'm not reproaching you for anything, my little

sister. I understand that your strolls through the apartment helped ease the strain.

CLAIRE [*irritated*]:

Ah! Stop it!

SOLANGE:

I want to help you. I want to comfort you, but I know I disgust you. I'm repulsive to you. And I know it because you disgust me. When slaves love one another, it's not love.

CLAIRE:

And me, I'm sick of seeing my image thrown back at me by a mirror, like a bad smell. You're my bad smell. Well, I'm ready. Ready to bite. I'll have my crown and I shall stroll about the apartment.

SOLANGE:

That's not reason enough to kill her.

CLAIRE:

Really? Why, please? For what other reason? Where and when could we find a better excuse? Ah, so it's not enough, not enough to be raped by a milkman who goes blithely through our garrets? Tonight Madame will witness our shame. Bursting with laughter, laughing until the tears roll down her face, with her flabby sighs. No. I shall have my crown. I shall be the poisoner that you failed to be. It's my turn now to dominate you!

SOLANGE:

But I never. . . .

CLAIRE:

Hand me the towel! Hand me the clothespins! Peel the onions! Scrape the carrots! Scrub the tiles! It's over. Over. Ah! I almost forgot! Turn off the tap! It's over. [*Exalted*] I'll run the world!

SOLANGE:

My little baby sister!

CLAIRE:

You'll help me.

SOLANGE:

You won't know what gestures to make. Things are more serious, Claire, and simpler too.

CLAIRE [*exalted*]:

We've read the story of Sister Holy Cross of the Blessed Valley who poisoned twenty-seven Arabs. She walked without shoes, with her feet all stiff. She was lifted up, carried off to the crime. We've read the story of Princess Albanarez who caused the death of her lover and her husband. She uncorked the bottle and made a big sign of the cross over the goblet. As she stood before the corpses, she saw only death and, off in the distance, the fleet image of herself being carried by the wind. She made all the gestures of earthly despair. In the book about the Marquise de Venosa, the one who poisoned her children, we're told that, as she approached the bed, her arms were supported by the ghost of her lover.

SOLANGE:

Baby sister, my angel!

CLAIRE:

I'll be supported by the sturdy arms of the milkman. I'll lean my left hand on the back of his neck. He won't flinch. You'll help me. And, far away, Solange, if we have to go far away, if I have to leave for Devil's Island, you'll come with me. You'll board the boat. The flight you were planning for him can be used for me. We shall be that eternal couple, Solange, the two of us, the eternal couple of the criminal and the saint. We'll be saved, Solange, saved, I swear to you! [*She falls on Madame's bed.*]

SOLANGE:

Be calm. You're going to sleep. I'll carry you upstairs.

CLAIRE:

Let me alone. Turn out the light. Please turn out the light. [SOLANGE *turns out the light.*]

SOLANGE:

Rest. Rest, little sister. [*She kneels, removes* CLAIRE'S *shoes, kisses her feet.*] Be calm, my darling. [*She caresses her.*] Put your feet on my shoulders. There. Close your eyes.

CLAIRE [*she sighs*]:

I'm ashamed, Solange.

SOLANGE [*very gently*]:

Don't talk. Leave things to me. I'm going to put you to bed and, when you fall asleep, I'll carry you upstairs, to the garret. I'll undress you and put you into your little cot. Sleep. I'll be here.

CLAIRE:

I'm ashamed, Solange.

SOLANGE:

Sh! Let me tell you a story.

CLAIRE [*simply*]:

Solange.

SOLANGE:

My angel?

CLAIRE:

Solange, listen....

SOLANGE:

Sleep. [*A long silence.*]

CLAIRE:

You have lovely hair. You have such lovely hair. Hers—

SOLANGE:

Don't talk about her any more.

CLAIRE:

Hers is false. [*A long silence.*] Do you remember? Under the tree, just the two of us? Our feet in the sun? Solange?

SOLANGE:

I'm here. Sleep. I'm your big sister.

[*Silence. A moment later* CLAIRE *gets up.*]

CLAIRE:

No! No weakness! Put the light on! Put it on! Quick! It's

too great a moment! [SOLANGE *puts the light on.*] Stand up. And let's eat. What's in the kitchen? Eh? We've got to eat. To be strong. Come along, you'll advise me. The phenobarbital.

SOLANGE:

I'm too exhausted. Yes, the phenobarbital.

CLAIRE:

The phenobarbital! Don't make such a face. We must be joyous. And sing. Let's sing! Sing, the way you'll sing when you go begging in the courts and embassies! Laugh! [*They burst out laughing.*] Otherwise, it'll be so tragic that we'll go flying out the window. Shut the window. [SOLANGE, *laughing, shuts the window.*] Murder is a thing that's . . . unspeakable!

SOLANGE:

Let's sing! We'll carry her off to the woods, and under the fir trees we'll cut her to bits by the light of the moon. And we'll sing. We'll bury her beneath the flowers, in our flower beds, and at night—we'll water her *toes* with a little *hose!* [*The front doorbell rings.*]

CLAIRE:

It's Madame!

SOLANGE:

It must be her! Straighten the bed. [*She seizes her sister by the wrists.*] Claire, are you sure you can go through with it?

CLAIRE:

How many do we need?

SOLANGE:

About ten. Put ten pills into her tea. Will you do it?

CLAIRE [*she frees herself, goes to tidy the bed, stares at it for a moment.*]: Yes. I've got the tube in my pocket.

[*Exit* SOLANGE, *left.* CLAIRE *continues tidying the room and leaves right. A few seconds elapse. A burst of nervous laughter backstage.* MADAME, *in a fur coat, enters laughing, with* SOLANGE *behind her.*]

MADAME:

There's no end to it! Such horrible gladioli, such a sickly pink, and mimosa! They probably hunt through the market before dawn to get them cheaper. [SOLANGE *helps her off with her coat.*]

SOLANGE:

Madame wasn't too cold?

MADAME:

Yes, Solange, I was very cold. I've been trailing through corridors all night long. I've been seeing frozen men and stony faces, but I did manage to catch a glimpse of Monsieur. From a distance. I waved to him. I've only just left the wife of a magistrate. Claire!

SOLANGE:

She's preparing Madame's tea.

MADAME:

I wish she'd hurry. I'm ashamed to ask for tea when Monsieur is all alone, without a thing, without food, without cigarettes.

66

SOLANGE:

But Monsieur won't stay there long. They'll see right away that he's not guilty.

MADAME:

Guilty or not, I shall never desert him, never. You see, Solange, it's at times like this that you realize how much you love someone. I don't think he's guilty either, but if he were, I'd become his accomplice. I'd follow him to Devil's Island, to Siberia.

SOLANGE:

There's no need to get panicky. I've seen worse cases acquitted. There was a trial in Bordeaux—

MADAME:

Do you go to trials? You?

SOLANGE:

I read the crime news. It was about a man who—

MADAME:

You can't compare Monsieur's case. He's been accused of the most idiotic thefts. I know he'll get out of it. All I mean is that, as a result of this preposterous affair, I've come to realize how deeply attached I am to him. Of course, none of this is serious, but if it were, Solange, it would be a joy for me to bear his cross. I'd follow him from place to place, from prison to prison, on foot if need be, as far as the penal colony.

SOLANGE:

They wouldn't let you. Only bandits' wives, or their sisters, or their mothers, are allowed to follow them.

MADAME:

A condemned man is no longer a bandit. And then I'd force my way in, past the guards. [*Suddenly conquettish*] And, Solange, I'd be utterly fearless. I'd use my weapons. What do you take me for?

SOLANGE:

Madame mustn't get such ideas into her head. You must rest.

MADAME:

I'm not tired. You treat me like an invalid. You're always ready to coddle me and pamper me as if I were dying. Thank God, I've got my wits about me. I'm ready for the fight. [*She looks at* SOLANGE *and, feeling that she has hurt her, adds, with a smile*] Come, come, don't make such a face. [*With sudden violence*] All right, it's true! There are times when you're so sweet that I simply can't stand it. It crushes me, stifles me! And those flowers which are there for the very opposite of a celebration!

SOLANGE:

If Madame means that we lack discretion. . . .

MADAME:

But I didn't mean anything of the kind, my dear girl. It's just that I'm so upset. You see what a state I'm in.

SOLANGE:

Would Madame like to see the day's accounts?

MADAME:

You certainly picked the right time. You must be mad. Do

you think I could look at figures now? Show them to me tomorrow.

SOLANGE [*putting away the fur cape*]:
The lining's torn. I'll take it to the furrier tomorrow.

MADAME:
If you like. Though it's hardly worth while. I'm giving up my wardrobe. Besides, I'm an old woman.

SOLANGE:
There go those gloomy ideas again.

MADAME:
I'm thinking of going into mourning. Don't be surprised if I do. How can I lead a worldly life when Monsieur is in prison? If you find the house too sad. . . .

SOLANGE:
We'll never desert Madame.

MADAME:
I know you won't, Solange. You've not been too unhappy with me, have you?

SOLANGE:
Oh!

MADAME:
When you needed anything, I saw that you got it. With my old gowns alone you both could have dressed like princesses. Besides . . . [*She goes to the closet and looks at her dresses*] of what use will they be to me? I'm through with finery and all that goes with it.

[CLAIRE *enters carrying the tea.*]

CLAIRE:

The tea is ready.

MADAME:

Farewell to parties and dances and the theater. You'll inherit all that.

CLAIRE:

Madame is losing her self-control. She must pull herself together.

SOLANGE:

The tea is ready.

MADAME:

Put it down. I'm going to bed. It's all over. [*She runs her hand over the red velvet dress.*] My lovely "Fascination," the loveliest of them all. [*She takes it down and runs her hand over it.*] It was designed for me by Chanel. Specially. Here, you may have it. It's yours. [*She gives it to* CLAIRE *and searches in the closet.*]

CLAIRE:

For me?

MADAME [*smiling sadly*]:

Of course. I said so, didn't I?

SOLANGE:

Madame is very kind. [*To* CLAIRE] You might thank Madam . You've been admiring it so long.

70

CLAIRE:

It's so beautiful. I'll never dare wear it.

MADAME:

You can have it altered. There's enough velvet in the train alone for the sleeves. And for you, Solange, I'm going to give you. . . . What shall I give you? Here, this coat. [*She hands* SOLANGE *the magnificent fur cape.*]

CLAIRE:

Oh! the fur cape!

SOLANGE [*thrilled*]:

Oh! Madame . . . never . . . Madame's too kind.

MADAME:

No, no, don't thank me. It's such a pleasure to make people happy. Now I'm going to get undressed. [*She looks at the telephone.*] Who left the receiver off?

CLAIRE:

It was Monsieur. . . . [*She stops suddenly.*]

MADAME [*dumbfounded*]:

Eh? Monsieur? [CLAIRE *is silent.*] What do you mean? Speak up!

SOLANGE [*slowly and as if in spite of herself*]:

When Monsieur rang up.

MADAME:

What are you talking about? Monsieur phoned?

SOLANGE:

We wanted to surprise Madame. Monsieur's out on bail.

He's waiting for Madame at the Hong-Kong Bar.

MADAME [*rising to her feet*]:
And you didn't say anything! Go get a taxi! Solange, quick, quick, get me a taxi. And hurry up. Go on, run. [*She pushes* SOLANGE *out of the room.*] My furs! Quick, quick! You're both mad. You let me go on talking. You really are mad. Or am *I* going mad! [*She puts on her fur coat. To* CLAIRE] When did he phone?

CLAIRE [*in a toneless voice*]:
Five minutes before Madame came in.

MADAME:
But you should have told me. And this cold tea! I'll never be able to wait for Solange to get back! Oh! What did he say?

CLAIRE:
What I've just told you. He was very calm.

MADAME:
Ah, him, he always is. He'd be utterly unconcerned if he were condemned to death. The man's unique! What else did he say?

CLAIRE:
Nothing. He said the judge was letting him out.

MADAME:
How can anyone leave police headquarters at midnight? Do judges work as late as that?

CLAIRE:
Sometimes, much later.

MADAME:

Much later? How do *you* know that?

CLAIRE:

I read *True Detective*. I know those things.

MADAME [*astonished*]:

Oh you do? You really are an odd little girl, Claire. She *might* hurry. [*She looks at her wrist watch.*] You won't forget to have the lining of my coat sewn?

CLAIRE:

I'll take it to the furrier tomorrow. [*A long silence.*]

MADAME:

What about the accounts? The day's accounts. Let me see them. I've got time!

CLAIRE:

Solange attends to that.

MADAME:

That's right. I'm all in a dither. I'll look at them tomorrow. [*Staring at* CLAIRE] Come a little closer! Come here! Why . . . you've got make-up on! [*Laughing*] Why Claire, you've been putting make-up on!

CLAIRE [*very embarrassed*]:

Madame. . . .

MADAME:

Ah, don't lie! Besides, you've every right to. Live, my child, live. In whose honor is it? Eh? Got a crush on someone? Own up!

CLAIRE:

I put a little powder on. . . .

MADAME:

That's not powder, it's make-up. But there's nothing wrong in that, you're still young. Make yourself attractive. Smarten up. [*She puts a flower in* CLAIRE's *hair. She looks at her wrist watch.*] What *can* she be doing? It's midnight and she's not back!

CLAIRE:

There aren't many taxis at this hour. She probably had to run to the cab-stand.

MADAME:

You think so? I've lost track of time. I'm wild with happiness. Monsieur ringing up at a time like that! And that he's free.

CLAIRE:

Madame ought to sit down. I'll go and heat up the tea. [*She starts to leave.*]

MADAME:

Don't bother, I'm not thirsty. It's champagne we'll be drinking tonight. You can be sure we won't be coming home.

CLAIRE:

Really, just a little tea. . . .

MADAME [*laughing*]:

I'm nervous enough as it is. I don't want you and Solange to wait up for us. Go upstairs and get to bed right away. [*Suddenly she sees the alarm clock.*] But. . . . That alarm clock, what's that doing here? Where does it come from?

CLAIRE [*very embarrassed*]:

The alarm clock? It's the kitchen clock.

MADAME:

It is? I've never seen it before.

CLAIRE [*she takes the alarm clock*]:

It belongs on the shelf. It's always been there.

MADAME [*smiling*]:

It's true I'm something of a stranger in the kitchen. You're
at home there. It's your domain. You're its sovereigns. But,
I wonder why you brought it in here?

CLAIRE:

It was Solange, for the cleaning. She'd never dare trust the
big clock.

MADAME:

How odd.

[CLAIRE *goes out carrying the alarm clock.*]

How odd. [*She looks at her wrist watch.*] She's certainly
taking her time. You can find taxis at every street-corner.
[*She sits down at her dressing table. She looks at herself
in the mirror and talks to herself.*] And what about you, you
fool, will you be beautiful enough to receive him? No
wrinkles, eh? It's been such a long separation, it'll have
been like a thousand years! Eh? Let's see, now. Gay?
Wistful? Idiot, you idiot, there I go talking to myself.
Happiness makes me giddy. And Solange not back yet. All
those flowers! Those girls do worship me, but—[*she*

looks at the top of the dressing table and blows at the powder] but they haven't dusted the dressing table. Their housekeeping is the most extraordinary combination of luxury and filth.

[*As she utters the last sentence,* CLAIRE *enters the room on tiptoe. She stands silently behind* MADAME *who suddenly notices her in the mirror.*] Eh? I'm raving, Claire, my mind's wandering. Forgive me. Today's been too dreadful.

CLAIRE:

Isn't Madame satisfied with our work?

MADAME [*smiling*]:

But I am, Claire. Delighted. In seventh heaven.

CLAIRE:

Madame's making fun of us.

MADAME [*laughing*]:

Oh, stop nagging me. After what I've been through today, I've got a right to be out of sorts. In the first place, there's that business of the letters to the police. . . . I wonder who could have sent them. I suppose you wouldn't have any idea?

CLAIRE:

Does Madame mean? . . .

MADAME:

I don't mean anything. I'd like to know, that's all. I've been groping around the whole day long as if I were blind. I felt like the police hunting in the bushes for a girl's corpse.

CLAIRE:

That's all over with. Monsieur is free.

MADAME:

Thank heavens. Which still doesn't account for those letters. What *can* she be doing? She's been gone an hour. Why didn't you tell me at once that Monsieur had phoned? He'll be furious.

CLAIRE:

We were terribly afraid of alarming Madame, of giving her a shock.

MADAME:

That was very bright. You're quietly killing me with flowers and kindness. One fine day I'll be found dead beneath the roses. Claire, what do you think of this coiffure? Do you like it?

CLAIRE:

If I might venture. . . .

MADAME:

Eh? If you might venture? Well, venture. I've full confidence in your opinion. Well? What do you think of it?

CLAIRE:

If I might be so bold as to make a suggestion, Madame's hair would look fluffier worn over the forehead.

MADAME:

Are you sure?

CLAIRE:

It would soften Madame's face.

MADAME:

Like that? You're right. You *are* a bright girl, Claire. You know, Claire, I've always thought you had a great deal of taste and that you were meant for better things.

CLAIRE:

I'm not complaining.

MADAME:

No, no, I know. But after all, you *are* more sensitive than the others. I realize that it's not much fun living with them. Fortunately you're with your sister. You're a family. But with a bit of luck you—

CLAIRE:

Oh! If I had wanted to!

MADAME:

I don't doubt it! [*She listens*] Listen! [*She stands up*] Listen! A car. It's her. Ah! [*She looks at herself again in the mirror.*]

CLAIRE:

Madame should have some tea because of the cold.

MADAME [*laughing*]:

You're trying to kill me with your tea and your flowers and your suggestions. You're too much for me, Claire. No. I've never felt so alive. Oh! And served in the best tea set, the *very best* set! Such pomp! Such elegance! [*She wants to leave, but* CLAIRE *stands between her and the door.*]

CLAIRE [*imploringly*]:

Madame *must* drink it. Otherwise. . . .

[SOLANGE *dashes in. She pushes her sister aside and turns to* MADAME.]

MADAME:

Well!

SOLANGE [*surprised*]:

Ah! Madame's still here. I've looked everywhere. No one wanted to come as late as this!

MADAME:

Did you get a taxi?

SOLANGE:

It's here, Madame. It's downstairs, Madame.

MADAME:

Let's hurry. So it's understood, you're to go upstairs and to bed. And tomorrow morning we'll just sleep and sleep and sleep. Claire, come and close the door behind me. And you're not to latch it.

[*She leaves, followed by* CLAIRE. SOLANGE *is left alone.* CLAIRE *returns. The two sisters look at one another.*]

SOLANGE [*ironically*]:

You certainly did a fine job. And you sneered at me.

CLAIRE:

Don't. I tried so hard not to say it, but I just couldn't help myself.

SOLANGE:

Didn't she drink it? [CLAIRE *shakes her head "no."*] Obviously. It was to be expected.

CLAIRE:

I'd have liked to see *you* in my place. [*She remains motionless for a moment and then starts walking toward the kitchen.*]

SOLANGE:

Where are you going?

CLAIRE [*without turning around and in a weary voice*]:

To sleep!

[*She leaves.*]

SOLANGE:

Claire! [*Silence.*] Claire! [*She goes to the door and calls her.*] Claire, I'm calling you.

CLAIRE [*off stage*]:

Who cares?

SOLANGE [*facing the door at the right*]:

Come here. Do you hear me? Come here.

[CLAIRE *comes in untying her apron.*]

CLAIRE [*very wearily*]:

What do you want? Is it my fault? The "tay"—as she says —was ready. I put in the pills. She wouldn't drink it!

SOLANGE:

And so you think we're just going to sit here and shake? [*She stares hard at her sister.*] They'll both be back tomorrow, drunk probably and vicious, like conquerors. They'll know where the letters came from. They—I hate her. [CLAIRE *shrugs her shoulders.*] Oh, I hate her! I loathe her! And you, you just stand there! Didn't you see how she sparkled? How disgustingly happy she was? *Her* joy feeds on *our* shame. Her carnation is the red of our shame. Her dress. . . . [*She kicks at the red velvet dress.*] It's the red of our shame. Her furs. . . . Ah! She took back her furs! And you just stand there! You don't scream. Are you dead?

CLAIRE:

What do you want me to do? She got away from us. You came back too soon.

SOLANGE:

She gets away and you just stand there!

CLAIRE:

What do you want to do? Make a scene? Eh? [*She screams in the face of* SOLANGE, *who remains motionless.*] You want to make a scene? Answer. Answer. Well, answer. We've got time. We've got all night.

SOLANGE [*in a very calm tone*]:

Let's get on with it.

CLAIRE:

What's the hurry? No, we'll take our time. Shall we? [*She unties her apron.*]

SOLANGE:

Keep your apron on. It's your turn.

CLAIRE:

No, that doesn't matter.

SOLANGE:

It's my turn to be Madame.

CLAIRE:

Take the apron.

SOLANGE:

But Claire....

CLAIRE [*simply*]:

I'm used to it. Here. [*She delicately hands the apron to*
SOLANGE.] Do you think I've really got too much rouge on?

SOLANGE:

Rouge? Yes, there's some rouge left. . . . But you're not
rouged. You're all made-up.

CLAIRE:

That's what she said.

SOLANGE:

That's all over. [*She grabs the apron.*] Forced to wear that!
But I want to be a real maid. [*She ties the strings behind
her back.*] Put out the light.

CLAIRE [*timidly*]:

You. . . . You don't want us to . . . to organize things in the
dark?

SOLANGE:

Do as I say. [*She puts out the light. The room is in semi-
darkness. The two sisters look at one another and speak,
without moving.*]

CLAIRE:

Oh! Let's wait a little while, Solange. Suppose she comes
back? Madame might have forgotten something. At times
like that one always forgets . . . one's bag, or money, or. . . .

SOLANGE:
Naive!

CLAIRE [*muttering*]:
She left in such a hurry. It's a trap. Madame suspects something.

SOLANGE [*shrugging her shoulders*]:
What? For instance?

CLAIRE:
She's suspicious. We're being watched. . . .

SOLANGE:
What of it? We're beyond that!

CLAIRE [*she wants to gain time*]:
You're not listening to me, Solange. I assure you, I feel something, I feel it. Listen, we're being spied on. I'm sure she'll come back unexpectedly. She'll have forgotten her handkerchief. Or her gloves. [SOLANGE *shrugs her shoulders.*] Or her compact, God knows what. But I feel there's something here, Solange—something in this room—that can record our gestures and play them back. Remember, Madame told us not to latch the front door. . . .

SOLANGE:
You're raving.

CLAIRE:
I'm not! No! Please, wait, please, it's so serious. Suppose she came back. . . .

SOLANGE:

Too bad for her!

CLAIRE:

You're growing terrible, Solange. You've got an answer for everything. At least. . . .

SOLANGE:

What?

CLAIRE [*timidly*]:

At least . . . suppose we said a prayer?

SOLANGE:

Do you dare bring God. . . .

CLAIRE:

But to the Holy. . . .

SOLANGE:

Bring the *Mother* of God into the ceremony? Really, you've got more nerve than I thought. You've no shame.

CLAIRE:

More softly, Solange, the walls are thin.

SOLANGE [*less loudly*]:

You're going mad, Claire. It's God who's listening to us. We know that it's for Him that the last act is to be performed, but we mustn't forewarn Him. We'll play it to the hilt.

CLAIRE:

Not so loud!

SOLANGE:
The walls are His ears.

CLAIRE:
Then I'll put on the white dress.

SOLANGE:
If you like. It makes no difference. But hurry up! Let's drop the preliminaries and get on with it. We've long since stopped needing the twists and turns and the lies. Let's get right into the transformation. Hurry up! Hurry up! I can't stand the shame and humiliation any longer. Who cares if the world listens to us and smiles and shrugs its shoulders and says I'm crazy and envious! I'm quivering, I'm shuddering with pleasure. Claire, I'm going to whinny with joy!

[*During this speech,* CLAIRE *has taken down the white dress and, hidden behind a screen, has put it on over her black dress whose black sleeves show.*]

CLAIRE [*appearing, all in white, with an imperious voice*]:
Begin!

SOLANGE [*ecstatically*]:
You're beautiful!

CLAIRE:
Skip that. You said we're skipping the prelude. Start the insults.

SOLANGE:
I'll never be able to. You dazzle me.

CLAIRE:

I said the insults! Let them come, let them unfurl, let them drown me, for, as you well know, I loathe servants. A vile and odious breed, I loathe them. They're not of the human race. Servants ooze. They're a foul effluvium drifting through our rooms and hallways, seeping into us, entering our mouths, corrupting us. I vomit you!

SOLANGE:

Go on. [*Silence.* CLAIRE *coughs*] Go on! I'm getting there, I'm getting there!

CLAIRE:

I know they're necessary, just as gravediggers and scavangers and policemen are necessary. Nevertheless, they're a putrid lot.

SOLANGE:

Go on, go on!

CLAIRE:

Your frightened guilty faces, your puckered elbows, your outmoded clothes, your wasted bodies, only fit for our cast-offs! You're our distorting mirrors, our loathsome vent, our shame, our dregs!

SOLANGE:

Go on, go on!

CLAIRE:

Please hurry. Please! I can't go on. You're . . . you're. . . . My God, I can't think of anything. My mind's a blank. I've run out of insults. Claire, you exhaust me.

SOLANGE:

Stop. I've got there. It's my turn.—Madame had her billing and cooing, her lovers, her milkman. . . .

CLAIRE:

Solange. . . .

SOLANGE:

Silence! Her morning milkman, her messenger of dawn, her handsome clarion, her pale and charming lover. That's over. [*She takes down a riding whip.*] Take your place for the ball.

CLAIRE:

What are you doing?

SOLANGE [*solemnly*]:

I'm checking the flow. Down on your knees!

CLAIRE:

Solange. . . .

SOLANGE:

Down on your knees! [CLAIRE *hesitates and kneels.*] Ah! Ah! You were so beautiful, the way you wrung your precious arms! Your tears, your petals oozed down your lovely face. Ah! Ah! Down! [CLAIRE *does not move.*] Down! [SOLANGE *strikes her.*] *Get down!* [CLAIRE *lies down.*] Ah! You amuse me, my dear! Crawl! Crawl, I say, like a worm! And you were going to follow in the wake of the boats, to cross the sea to aid and comfort your handsome exile! Look at yourself again! That role is only for the fairest of the fair. The guards would snicker. People would point at you. Your

lover would hang his head in shame! And are you strong
enough? Strong enough to carry his bag? And spry enough,
Madame, spry enough on your feet? Don't worry. I'm not
jealous. I don't need that thief where I'm going. No, Madame. I myself am both the thief and his slavish shadow.
I move alone toward the brightest shores.

CLAIRE:
I'm losing him!

SOLANGE:
Aren't I enough for you?

CLAIRE:
Solange, please, I'm sinking.

SOLANGE:
Sink! But rise again to the surface. I know what my final
destiny is to be. I've reached shelter. I can be bountiful.
[*She takes a breath.*] Stand up! I'll marry you standing up!
Ah! Ah! Groveling on the rug at a man's feet. What a sorry,
facile gesture. The great thing is to end in beauty. How are
you going to get up?

CLAIRE [*getting up slowly and clumsily*]:
You're killing me.

SOLANGE [*ironically*]:
Careful now, watch your movements.

CLAIRE [*on her feet*]:
We're out of our depth. We must go to bed. My throat's—

SOLANGE [*striding up to her*]:
Madame has a very lovely throat. The throat of a queen. [CLAIRE *moves back to the kitchen door.*] Of a dove. Come, my turtle dove!

CLAIRE [*she withdraws farther back, putting her hands to her neck as if to protect it*]:
It's late.

SOLANGE:
Never too late.

CLAIRE:
Madame. . . .

SOLANGE:
. . . is drinking champagne with Monsieur who has returned from the dead.

CLAIRE:
She'll be back any moment. Let me go.

SOLANGE:
Stop worrying. She's waltzing! She's waltzing! She's guzzling fine wine! She's delirious.

CLAIRE:
Let's get out of here, Solange. I tell you we're in danger.

SOLANGE:
Go into the vestry. [*She points to the kitchen door*] Go on in. You've got to finish the linoleum.

CLAIRE [*she screams in a hollow voice*]:
Help!

SOLANGE:

Don't yell! It's useless. Death is present, and is stalking you. Don't yell! I, who kept you the way they keep kittens for drowning. I, yes I, who trimmed my belly with pins to stab all the foetuses I threw into the gutter! In order to keep you, to have *you* alive!

CLAIRE [*running about the room*]:

Solange, Solange, come to yourself!

SOLANGE [*running after her*]:

To *yourself*!

CLAIRE [*in a dull voice*]:

Help!

SOLANGE:

Stop yelling! No one can hear you! We're both beyond the pale.

CLAIRE:

Solange....

SOLANGE:

Everyone's listening, but no one will hear.

CLAIRE:

I'm ill....

SOLANGE:

You'll be taken care of there.

CLAIRE:

I'm ill ... I ... I'm going to be sick.... [*She seems to be gagging.*]

SOLANGE [*she approaches her and says sympathetically*]:
Really? Are you really ill? Claire, are you really feeling
ill?

CLAIRE:
I'm, I'm going to—

SOLANGE:
Not here, Claire, hold it in. [*She supports her.*] Not here,
please, please. Come. Lean on me. There. Walk gently.
We'll be better off there, in our flowered domain. I have
such sure ways of putting an end to all suffering.
[*They leave by the kitchen door. The stage remains empty
for a few seconds. A gust of wind opens the unlocked window. Enter* SOLANGE, *right, wearing her short black dress.
Throughout the scene she will seem to be addressing characters who are imaginary, though present.*]

SOLANGE:
Madame. . . . At last! Madame is dead! . . . laid out on the
linoleum . . . strangled by the dish-gloves. What? Oh, Madame may remain seated. . . . Madame may call me Mademoiselle Solange. . . . Exactly. It's because of what I've
done. Madame and Monsieur will call me Mademoiselle
Solange Lemercier. . . . Madame should have taken off that
black dress. It's grotesque. [*She imitates Madame's voice.*]
So I'm reduced to wearing mourning for my maid. As I left
the cemetery all the servants of the neighborhood marched
past me as if I were a member of the family. I've so often
been part of the family. Death will see the joke through to

the bitter end. . . . What? Oh! Madame needn't feel sorry for me. I'm Madame's equal and I hold my head high. . . . Oh! And there are things Monsieur doesn't realize. He doesn't know that he used to obey our orders. [*She laughs*] Ah! Ah! Monsieur was a tiny little boy. Monsieur toed the line when we threatened. No, Inspector, no. . . . I won't talk! I won't say a word. I refuse to speak about our complicity in this murder. . . . The dresses? Oh, Madame could have kept them. My sister and I had our own. Those we used to put on at night, in secret. Now, I have my own dress, and I'm your equal. I wear the red garb of criminals. Monsieur's laughing at me? He's smiling at me. Monsieur thinks I'm mad. He's thinking maids should have better taste than to make gestures reserved for Madame! Monsieur really forgives me? Monsieur is the soul of kindness. He'd like to vie with me in grandeur. But I've scaled the fiercest heights. Madame now sees my loneliness—at last! Yes, I am alone. And fearsome. I might say cruel things, but I can be kind. . . . Madame will get over her fright. She'll get over it well enough. What with her flowers and perfumes and gowns and jewels and lovers. As for me, I've my sister. . . . Yes. I dare speak of these things. I do, Madame. There's nothing I won't dare. And who could silence me, who? Who would be so bold as to say to me: "My dear child!" I've been a servant. Well and good. I've made the gestures a servant must make. I've smiled at Madame. I've bent down to make the bed, bent down to scrub the tiles, bent down to peel vegetables, to listen at doors, to glue my eye to keyholes! But now I stand upright. And firm. I'm the strangler. Mademoiselle Solange, the one who strangled her sister! . . . Me be still? Madame is delicate, really. But I pity Madame. I pity Madame's whiteness, her satiny skin, and her little ears, and little wrists. . . . Eh? I'm the black crow. . . . Oh! Oh! I have my judges. I belong to the police. Claire? She was really very fond of Madame. . . . YOUR dresses again! And THAT white dress, THAT one, which I forbade her to put on, the one you wore the night of the Opera Ball, the night you poked fun at her, because she was sitting in the kitchen admiring a photo of Gary Cooper. . . . Madame will remember. Madame will remember her gentle irony, the maternal grace with which she took the magazine from us, and smiled. Nor will Madame forget that she called her Clarinette. Monsieur laughed until the tears rolled down his cheeks. . . . Eh? Who am I? The monstrous soul of servantdom! . . . No, Inspector, I'll explain nothing in their presence. That's *our* business. It would be a fine thing if masters could pierce the shadows where servants live. . . . That, my child, is our darkness, ours. [*She lights a cigarette and smokes clumsily. The smoke makes her cough.*] Neither you nor anyone else will be told anything. Just tell yourselves that this time Solange has gone through with it. . . . You see her dressed in red. She is going out. [*She goes to the window, opens it, and steps out on the balcony. Facing the night, with her back to the audience, she delivers the following speech. A slight breeze makes the curtains stir.*] Going out. Descending the great stairway.

Accompanied by the police. Out on your balconies to see her making her way among the shadowy penitents! It's noon. She's carrying a nine-pound torch. The hangman follows close behind. He's whispering sweet nothings in her ear. Claire! The hangman's by my side! Now take your hand off my waist. He's trying to kiss me! Let go of me! Ah! Ah! [*She laughs.*] The hangman's trifling with me. She will be led in procession by all the maids of the neighborhood, by all the servants who accompanied Claire to her final resting place. They'll all be wearing crowns, flowers, streamers, banners. They'll toll the bell. The funeral will unfold its pomp. It's beautiful, isn't it? First come the butlers, in full livery, but without silk lining. They're wearing their crowns. Then come the footmen, the lackeys in knee breeches and white stockings. They're wearing their crowns. Then come the valets, and then the chambermaids wearing our colors. Then the porters. And then come the delegations from heaven. And I'm leading them. The hangman's lulling me. I'm being acclaimed. I'm pale and I'm about to die. . . . [*She returns to the room.*] And what flowers! They gave her such a lovely funeral, didn't they? Oh! Claire, poor little Claire! [*She bursts into tears and collapses into an armchair*] What? [*She gets up.*] It's no use, Madame, I'm obeying the police. They're the only ones who understand me. They too belong to the world of outcasts, the world you touch only with tongs.

[*Visible only to the audience, Claire, during the last few moments, has been leaning with her elbows against the jamb*

of the kitchen door and listening to her sister.]
Now we are Mademoiselle Solange Lemercier, that Lemercier woman. The famous criminal. And above all, Monsieur need not be uneasy. I'm not a maid. I have a noble soul. . . . [*She shrugs her shoulders*] No, no, not another word, my dear fellow. Ah, Madame's not forgetting what I've done for her. . . . No, no she must not forget my devotion. . . .

[*Meanwhile* CLAIRE *enters through the door at the left. She is wearing the white dress.*]

And in spite of my forbidding it, Madame continues to stroll about the apartment. She will please sit down . . . and listen to me. . . . [*To* CLAIRE] Claire . . . we're raving!

CLAIRE [*complainingly, Madame's voice*]:
You're talking far too much, my child. Far too much. Shut the window. [SOLANGE *shuts the window.*] Draw the curtains. Very good, Claire!

SOLANGE:
It's late. Everyone's in bed. . . . We're playing an idiotic game.

CLAIRE [*she signals with her hand for silence*]:
Claire, pour me a cup of tea.

SOLANGE:
But. . . .

CLAIRE:
I said a cup of tea.

SOLANGE:

We're dead-tired. We've got to stop. [*She sits down in an armchair.*]

CLAIRE:

Ah, by no means! Poor servant girl, you think you'll get out of it as easily as that? It would be too simple to conspire with the wind, to make the night one's accomplice. Solange, you will contain me within you. Now pay close attention.

SOLANGE:

Claire. . . .

CLAIRE:

Do as I tell you. I'm going to help you. I've decided to take the lead. Your role is to keep me from backing out, nothing more.

SOLANGE:

What more do you want? We're at the end. . . .

CLAIRE:

We're at the very beginning.

SOLANGE:

They'll be coming. . . .

CLAIRE:

Forget about them. We're alone in the world. Nothing exists but the altar where one of the two maids is about to immolate herself—

SOLANGE:

But—

CLAIRE:

Be still. It will be your task, yours alone, to keep us both alive. You must be very strong. In prison no one will know that I'm with you, secretly. On the sly.

SOLANGE:

I'll never be able. . . .

CLAIRE:

Please, stand up straight. Up straight, Solange! Claire! Darling, stand straight now. Up straight. Pull yourself together.

SOLANGE:

You're overwhelming me.

CLAIRE:

A staff! A standard! Claire, up straight! I call upon you to represent me—

SOLANGE:

I've been working too hard. I'm exhausted.

CLAIRE:

To represent me in the world. [*She tries to lift her sister and keep her on her feet.*] My darling, stand up straight.

SOLANGE:

Please, I beg of you.

CLAIRE [*domineeringly*]:

I beg of you, stand up straight. Solemnly, Claire! Pretty does it, pretty does it! Up Claire! Up on your paws! [*She holds her by the wrists and lifts her from her chair.*] Up on your paws! Now then! Up! Up!

SOLANGE:
You don't realize the danger—

CLAIRE:
But, Solange, you're immortal! Repeat after me—

SOLANGE:
Talk. But not so loud.

CLAIRE [*mechanically*]:
Madame must have her tea.

SOLANGE [*firmly*]:
No, I won't.

CLAIRE [*holding her by the wrists*]:
You bitch! Repeat. Madame must have her tea.

SOLANGE:
I've just been through such a lot. . . .

CLAIRE [*more firmly*]:
Madame will have her tea. . . .

SOLANGE:
Madame will have her tea. . . .

CLAIRE:
Because she must sleep. . . .

SOLANGE:
Because she must sleep. . . .

CLAIRE:
And I must stay awake.

SOLANGE:
And I must stay awake.

CLAIRE [*she lies down on Madame's bed*]:
Don't interrupt again. I repeat. Are you listening? Are you obeying? [SOLANGE *nods "yes."*] I repeat: My tea!

SOLANGE [*hesitating*]:
But. . . .

CLAIRE:
I say: my tea.

SOLANGE:
But, Madame.

CLAIRE:
Good. Continue.

SOLANGE:
But, Madame, it's cold.

CLAIRE:
I'll drink it anyway. Let me have it. [SOLANGE *brings the tray.*] And you've poured it into the best, the finest tea set. [*She takes the cup and drinks, while* SOLANGE, *facing the audience, delivers the end of her speech.*]

SOLANGE:
The orchestra is playing brilliantly. The attendant is raising the red velvet curtain. He bows. Madame is descending the stairs. Her furs brush against the green plants. Madame steps into the car. Monsieur is whispering sweet nothings in her ear. She would like to smile, but she is dead. She rings the bell. The porter yawns. He opens the door. Madame goes up the stairs. She enters her apartment—but,

Madame is dead. Her two maids are alive: they've just risen up, free, from Madame's icy form. All the maids were present at her side—not they themselves, but rather the hellish agony of their names. And all that remains of them to float about Madame's airy corpse is the delicate perfume of the holy maidens which they were in secret. We are beautiful, joyous, drunk, and free!

CURTAIN

DEATHWATCH

A Play in One Act

Deathwatch (Haute Surveillance) was published by the Librairie Gallimard in 1949. The text, however, was greatly altered by the author in the course of rehearsal. The present translation follows the acting version, which supersedes the published text.

Though published and produced after *The Maids, Deathwatch* is Jean Genet's first play. It was performed for the first time at the Théâtre des Mathurins in Paris on February 24, 1949, and was directed by the author. The set and costumes were designed by André Beaurepaire. The cast was as follows:

Green Eyes	Tony Taffin
Maurice	Claude Romain
Lefranc	Robert Hossein
The Guard	Jean-Marc Lambert

THE CHARACTERS

GREEN EYES:	22 years old (his feet chained).
MAURICE:	17 years old.
LEFRANC:	23 years old.
THE GUARD	

DEATHWATCH

SETTING

A prison cell.

The walls of the cell are of hewn stone and should give the impression that the architecture of the prison is very complicated. Rear, a barred transom, the spikes of which turn inward. The bed is a block of granite on which a few blankets are heaped. Right, a barred door.

*

SOME DIRECTIONS

The entire play unfolds as in a dream. The set and costumes (striped homespun) should be in violent colors. Use whites and very hard blacks, clashing with each other. The movements of the actors should be either heavy or else extremely and incomprehensibly rapid, like flashes of lightning. If they can, the actors should deaden the timbre of their voices. Avoid clever lighting. As much light as possible. The text is given in the ordinary language of conversation and is correctly spelled, but the actors should recite it with the characteristic deformations that go with the accent of the slums. The actors walk silently, on felt soles. Maurice is barefoot.

Whenever Maurice utters the name Green Eyes, he drawls it.

*

When the curtain rises, GREEN EYES *is holding* LEFRANC *and pulling him gently back so as to get him away from* MAURICE *who is somewhat frightened and straightening his clothes*

GREEN EYES [*softly*]:
You're crazy. You're a pair of lunatics. I'll calm both of you with a single smack. I'll lay you both out on the cement. [*To* LEFRANC] Another second and Maurice would have got it. Watch out with your hands, Georgie. Stop the big act, and stop talking about the Negro.
LEFRANC [*violently*]:
It's him. . . .
GREEN EYES:
It's you. [*He hands him a sheet of paper*] Go on reading.

LEFRANC:

Let him keep his mouth shut.

GREEN EYES:

It's you, Georgie. Stop annoying us. I don't want to hear any more about Snowball. Neither he nor the guys in his cell bother about us. [*He listens*] Visiting hours have started. It'll be my turn in a quarter of an hour.

[*During the following scene he keeps pacing up and down*]

MAURICE [*pointing to* LEFRANC]:

He's always trying to make trouble. There'll never be any peace with him around. For him, no one matters. Only Snowball.

LEFRANC [*violently*]:

Yes, Snowball. You said it. He's got what it takes. Don't play around with him. He's a Negro, a savage . . .

MAURICE:

Nobody . . .

LEFRANC:

He's a savage, a Negro, but he shoots lightning. Green Eyes . . .

MAURICE:

What?

LEFRANC [*to* GREEN EYES]:

Green Eyes, Snowball's got it all over you.

MAURICE:

You starting again? It's because this morning, on the way

105

up from recreation, he smiled at you in the hall.

LEFRANC:

At me? That sure would surprise me all right.

[GREEN EYES *turns around, stops and stares first at* LE-FRANC, *then at* MAURICE]

MAURICE:

There were just the three of us. If it wasn't at the guard, it was at one of us.

LEFRANC:

When was it?

MAURICE:

Ah ha? So you're interested? Just before we got to the middle circle. Oh! [*A faint smile*] Just a little wisp of a smile. He was winded from the four flights.

LEFRANC:

And what do you make of it?

MAURICE:

That you're one who causes all the trouble in this cell.

LEFRANC:

Maybe. But just let Snowball let out a snort and you guys vanish. He outclasses everyone. No one can get him down, no convict can outshine him. He's a real bruiser and he's been around.

MAURICE:

Who's denying it? He's a good-looking kid. As handsome as they come. And well-built. You might even call him a Green

Eyes with a coat of shoe-polish, Green Eyes with a smoke-screen, Green Eyes covered with mud, Green Eyes in the dark . . .

LEFRANC:

And Green Eyes isn't in the same class! You want me to tell you about Snowball?

MAURICE:

And what about the way Green Eyes answered the inspector?

LEFRANC:

Snowball? He's out of this world. All the guys in his cell feel it. And in the cells around too, and the whole prison and all the prisons in France. He shines. He beams. He's black but he lights up the whole two thousand cells. No one'll ever get him down. He's the real boss of the prison. All you've got to do is see him walk. . . .

MAURICE:

If Green Eyes wanted . . .

LEFRANC:

You haven't watched them! Just to see him, the way he goes through the halls, miles and miles of halls, with his chains. And what happens? His chains carry him. Snowball's a king. Maybe he comes from the jungle, but he comes with his head up! And his crimes! Compared to them, what Green Eyes did . . .

GREEN EYES: [*stopping, a gentle look on his face*]:

That'll do, Georgie. I'm not trying to pass myself off as

a king. In prison, no one's a king, Snowball no more than the next guy. Don't think I'm taken in by him. His talk about crimes may be just a lot of hot air!

LEFRANC:
Hot air!

MAURICE [*to* LEFRANC]:
Don't interrupt him. [*Listening at the door*] It's almost time for the visit. The guards are at 38.
[*He strides about the cell clockwise*]

GREEN EYES:
Hot air. I don't know anything about his crimes. . . .

LEFRANC:
The attack on the gold-train. . . .

GREEN EYES [*still curtly*]:
I don't know anything about them. I've got my own.

MAURICE:
Your own? You've got only one.

GREEN EYES:
If I say "my crimes," it's because I know what I'm saying. I say "my crimes." And no comments or I might get nasty. Better not needle me. All I'm asking you is one thing. Read me my girl's letter.

LEFRANC:
I've read it.

GREEN EYES:

What else does she say?

LEFRANC:

Nothing. I've read it all!

GREEN EYES [*he points to a passage in the letter*]:

All right, you read it all. But what about that? You didn't read that.

LEFRANC:

Don't you trust me?

GREEN EYES [*stubbornly*]:

But what about that?

LEFRANC:

What "that"? Tell me what it is.

GREEN EYES:

Georgie, you're taking advantage because I'm illiterate.

LEFRANC:

If you don't trust me, take it back. And don't ever expect me to read you your girl's letters again.

GREEN EYES:

Georgie, you defying me and there's going to be trouble. Watch your step, or somebody in this cell's going to be taken for a joyride.

LEFRANC:

You make me sick, Green Eyes. I'm telling you straight—I read it all. But I know you don't trust me any more. Maybe

109

you think I'm giving you the runaround with her. Don't listen to what Maurice says. He's egging us on.

MAURICE [*banteringly*]:

Me? The most peaceful kid. . . .

GREEN EYES [*to* LEFRANC]:

You're pulling a fast one on me.

LEFRANC:

Then go write your own letters!

GREEN EYES:

You bastard.

MAURICE [*gently*]:

Oh, Green Eyes, stop making a fuss. You'll see your girl again. You're too good-looking. You've got her in the palm of your hand. Where do you expect her to go?

GREEN EYES [*after a long silence, gently, almost regretfully*]:

You bastard.

MAURICE:

Don't get worked up. That's how Georgie is. He likes mystery and he's impressed by you.

LEFRANC:

All right, I'll tell you what there was in the letter. If you see your girl in the visitors' room later, ask her the truth. You want me to read? [GREEN EYES *neither answers nor moves*] Listen, your girl has caught on that you're not the one who's been writing. Now she thinks you can't read or write.

MAURICE:

If Green Eyes can treat himself to a writer, that's *his* business.

LEFRANC:

You want me to read? [*He reads*] "Darling, I realize it couldn't have been you who wrote those nice phrases, but I'd rather have you write yourself as best you can. . . ."

GREEN EYES:

You bastard!

LEFRANC:

Are you accusing me?

GREEN EYES:

You bastard! So that's it! She's getting ready to pull out on me. And you, you fixed it so she'd think the letters came from you.

LEFRANC:

You're crazy. I've always written what you told me.

MAURICE [*to* LEFRANC]:

You're smart all right, but Green Eyes can still let you have it. The gentleman was working in secret.

LEFRANC:

Stop making things worse, Maurice. I didn't try to humiliate him.

GREEN EYES:

Humiliate me? Stop kidding yourself. And don't think you humiliate me either when you claim that the nigger's a more dangerous guy. When it comes to niggers, I . . . [*he makes an obscene gesture*]. And tell me, what kept you from reading it to me? Answer. It's because you're making a play for my girl. Admit it. Because when you get out of here, in three days, you're hoping to shack up with her.

LEFRANC:

Listen, Green Eyes, you won't believe me. It was so as not to upset you. I'd have told you, but [*he points to* MAURICE] not in front of him.

GREEN EYES:

Why?

MAURICE:

Me? You should have said so. If I bother you, I can still vanish into the fog. I'm the kid who slips through walls. Everyone knows that. No, no, Georgie, no, you're handing us a line. Admit that you wanted his girl and we'll believe you.

LEFRANC [*violently*]:

Maurice, don't start complicating things again. You're a mischief maker. It's on account of you that there's trouble. You're a devil.

MAURICE:

O.K., you're bigger than me, go on, take it out on me, you've been picking fights for the past week. But you're wasting your time. I'll see to it that Green Eyes and I stay friends.

112

LEFRANC:

You're the ones. it's *you* who're against *me*. You don't let me live any more.

MAURICE:

Just before, when you grabbed me by the collar, you wanted to flatten me out. I felt myself turning purple. If it hadn't been for Green Eyes, I'd have got it. I owe my life to him, to Green Eyes. It's a good thing you're getting out. We'll have some peace.

LEFRANC:

Enough of that, Maurice.

MAURICE:

You see? You see, Georgie? I can't say a word. You'd like to squelch us, both of us. Not on your life, Georgie Lefranc.

LEFRANC:

There's no danger in your calling me George.

MAURICE:

He's used to calling you George. You ought to let us know instead of getting riled. You're trying to squelch us.

LEFRANC:

I do what I have to do.

MAURICE:

To who? Us two, we're staying locked up, and what you have to do is respect us. But you look as if you were plotting something. All by yourself. Because you *are* all by yourself, and don't forget it.

LEFRANC:

And what about you? What are you after with those gestures of yours? In front of him. And in front of the guards. You can try to get around them, but you won't get anywhere with me. If you got out of it before, it was on account of the faces you made. That's what saved you, more than Green Eyes. I took pity on you. But you'll get yours. And before I leave here.

MAURICE:

- Come on, Georgie, get tough. Come on, right now, while I'm looking at you. Just before you tried to kill me, but there are nights when you slip me your blankets, too. I noticed it long ago. And so did Green Eyes. *That* gave us a laugh *too*.

LEFRANC:

There's a lot you don't know about me if you think I was willing to sacrifice myself, especially for your carcass.

MAURICE:

You think I need that? You trying to be nice to me? And you think you'll disgust me any the less? Good thing you're leaving the cell in three days.

LEFRANC:

Don't count on it too much, Maurice. You're the one who'll be leaving. Before you came, everything was fine. Green Eyes and I got along like two men. I didn't talk about him as if he were a bride.

MAURICE:

You nauseate me!

114

[MAURICE *flicks his head as if tossing back an exasperating lock of hair*]

LEFRANC:

Stop that! I can't stand you any more! Everything you do gets on my nerves. I don't want to remember a single thing about you when I get out of here.

MAURICE:

What if I won't stop? You resent me because I haven't been in prison long. You'd have got a kick out of seeing my hair fall from the clippers, wouldn't you?

LEFRANC:

Shut it, Maurice!

MAURICE:

You'd have loved to see me sitting on the stool with my curls falling on my shoulders, on my lap, on the floor. You'd have loved it, wouldn't you? You even love to hear me talk about it, you love to see me in a rage. You get a real kick out of seeing me suffer.

LEFRANC:

I'm fed up being between you, fed up feeling your gestures pass through me when you talk to each other. I'm fed up with the sight of your little mugs. I know all about your winks. You wear me out. It's not enough to be dying of hunger, to be shut up lifeless in a cell. We've got to kill each other off as well.

MAURICE:

Are you trying to make me feel sorry for you by reminding me that you give me half your bread? And half your soup?

115

You can keep them. It was an effort to swallow the stuff. The mere fact that it came from you was enough to turn my stomach.

LEFRANC:

That's probably why you slipped some of it to Green Eyes occasionally.

MAURICE:

You'd have liked him to die of hunger.

LEFRANC:

I don't give a damn. Divvy it up if you like. I'm big enough to feed the whole cell.

MAURICE:

You can keep your soup, you poor martyr. I can still give half of mine to Green Eyes.

LEFRANC:

Fine. I'm glad you're building up his strength. But don't try to put one over on me. I'm way ahead of you.

MAURICE [*ironically*]:

On the galley?

LEFRANC:

Repeat that.

MAURICE:

I said: on the galley.

LEFRANC:

You trying to needle me, Maurice? You want to work me up? You want me to let you have it again?

MAURICE:

No one's saying anything against you. *You* started, by talking about the marks on your wrists. . . .

LEFRANC:

And on my ankles! That's right, Maurice. On my wrists and ankles. And I've got a right to talk. And you, to shut up! [*He screams*] Yes, I've got a right to! I've got a right to talk about it. For three hundred years I've borne the marks of a galley-slave, and it's going to end in trouble! You hear me? I can become a cyclone and tear you apart! And wipe up the cell! That sweetness of yours is killing me. One of us is going to clear out. You hear me, Maurice, you're wearing me down, you and your fine murderer!

MAURICE:

You see? You're accusing him again. You accuse him whenever you can so as to try to cover up your own sneaky ways. But we know you tried to steal his girl. The way you get up at night to steal tobacco. If we offer you any during the day, you refuse it. So as to be able to swipe it by moonlight. His girl! You've been itching for her for a long time.

LEFRANC:

You'd like me to say I have, wouldn't you? It'd make you happy? You'd enjoy seeing me on the outs with Green Eyes? All right, I have. You guessed right, Maurice, I have. I've been doing all I can for a long time to get her to drop him.

MAURICE:

You bastard!

LEFRANC:

I've been trying to get him away from her for a long time.
I don't give a damn about his girl. You understand? Not a
God damn. I wanted Green Eyes to be all alone. Solo, like
he says. But it isn't easy. He won't buckle. He stands his
ground. Maybe I botched it, but I don't admit I'm licked.

MAURICE:

What do you want to do with him? Where are you trying to
lead him? [*To* GREEN EYES] Green Eyes, you hear him?

LEFRANC:

None of your business. It's between us two. I'll keep at it
even if I have to change cells. And even if I leave prison.

MAURICE:

Green Eyes!

LEFRANC:

And I'll tell you something else—you're jealous. You can't
bear the fact that I'm the one who writes to his girl. I've
got too good a job. An important post—I'm the post-office.
And it drives you wild!

MAURICE [*teeth clenched*]:

It's not true.

LEFRANC:

Not true? If only you could hear yourself say it! You've
got tears in your eyes. Whenever I sat down at the table,
when I took a sheet of paper, when I unscrewed the bottle of
ink, you couldn't sit still. It's not true? You were all hopped
up, there was no holding you. And when I was writing? You

should have watched yourself. And when I reread the letter? You didn't hear yourself snicker, you didn't see the way your eyes were blinking.

MAURICE:

You wrote to her as if you were writing to your own girl! You poured out your heart on the paper!

LEFRANC:

But it was you who suffered! And you're still suffering! You're getting ready to cry! I'm making you cry with shame and fury! And I'm not done yet! Wait till he comes back from the visitors' room! He'll come back with smiles all over his face because he saw his girl.

MAURICE:

It's not true!

LEFRANC:

You think so! His girl couldn't forget him that easily. People don't forget Green Eyes! He's too much of a coward to leave her. Can't you just see him, eh? He's glued to the grate of the visitors' room. His life's starting all over again. . . .

MAURICE:

You bastard!

LEFRANC:

Don't you realize that you don't count? That he's the man! At this moment he's clinging to the grate. Look at him. He's stepping back so his girl can see him better! Just look at him!

119

MAURICE:

You're jealous! Jealous! You'd have liked them to talk about you all over France the way they talked about Green Eyes. It was wonderful. You know how wonderful it was when they couldn't find the corpse. The farmers were all out looking for it. The cops, the dogs! They drained wells, ponds. It was a real revolution. The whole world was out looking! Priests, well-diggers! And later, when they found it! The earth, the whole earth was fragrant with it. And what about Green Eyes' hands? His blood-stained hands, when he pushed aside the window-curtain? And when he shook her hair that was full of lilacs. The way he told us.

GREEN EYES [*stupefied*]:

Blood, Maurice? God damn it!

MAURICE:

What'd you say?

GREEN EYES:

Not blood, lilacs. [*He moves forward threateningly*]

MAURICE:

What lilacs?

GREEN EYES:

Between her teeth! In her hair. And it's only now that you tell me! [*He slaps* MAURICE] But not a single cop told me. I should have thought of it, and it's just my luck to think of it too late. [*To* MAURICE] And it's your fault, you rat. You should have been there. You were supposed to be there so as to warn me, but you manage so as to do it when it was all over, when I'm locked up, face to face with my regrets. You should have been on the spot but you were probably busy with my girl.

MAURICE:

Green Eyes. . . .

GREEN EYES:

I'm sick of all of you. You no longer exist. In a month I'll get the axe. My head'll be on one side of the block and my body on the other. I'm a terror, a holy terror! And I can blot you out. If you like my girl, go take her. I knew it. You've been circling around me for a long time, circling round, circling round, circling round, you've been trying to find a spot to land on, without even suspecting I can bash your head in.

MAURICE [*listening at the door*]:

Green Eyes . . . it's not too late. All you've got to do is show yourself and you'll get her back. Listen! Listen! They're at 34.

GREEN EYES:

No, let her begin a new life. She's right. I'll do like her. Starting here and ending on the other side of the water. If I get there! Only, she's going to tell me so in a little while, without ceremony. She's going to let me down in cold blood without realizing that if she waited another two months she'd be a widow. She could have come and prayed at my grave and brought . . . [*he hesitates*] . . . flowers. . . .

MAURICE [*tenderly*]:
Green Eyes. . . .

GREEN EYES:
A widow, I say! My little widow!

MAURICE:
Green Eyes . . . look, big boy. . . .

GREEN EYES:
My widow! And me, I'm a dead man! I make you laugh,
don't I? She despises me and fate abandons me and I don't
hit the ceiling. Now I realize. I'm a rag. A dish-mop! You'd
like to see me cry, Georgie, wouldn't you? Or throw a fit?
No, I'm sure my girl doesn't interest you.

LEFRANC:
She'll come. The visits have only just begun.
[*He goes to take a jacket hanging from a nail*]

MAURICE:
That's not your jacket. It's Green Eyes'.

LEFRANC [*putting the jacket back*]:
You're right. I made a mistake.

MAURICE:
It's been happening pretty often. That's the fifth or sixth
time you've put on his jacket.

LEFRANC:
What's the harm? There are no secrets, they don't have
pockets. [*A pause*] Say, Maurice, are you in charge of
Green Eyes' clothes?

MAURICE [*shrugging his shoulders*]:

That's *my* business!

GREEN EYES:

My little woman! The little bitch! She leaves me all alone in the middle of the desert. You just up and beat it, you fly away!

MAURICE:

I swear that if I ever run into her, I'll bump her off.

GREEN EYES:

Too late. As soon as you lay eyes on her, you'll forget all about Green Eyes.

MAURICE:

Never!

GREEN EYES:

Never say never. I know all about friends who swear they'll do things. You mustn't even touch her. She's just a poor kid. She needs a man, a real one, and I'm a ghost already. I should have known how to write. I ought to have made fine phrases. But *I'm* a fine phrase.

MAURICE:

So you forgive her?

GREEN EYES:

She doesn't deserve it, but what can I do?

MAURICE:

Bump her off. She ought to be bumped off. We've got guts in this cell.

GREEN EYES:

You make me laugh, both of you. Don't you see my situation? Can't you see that here we make up stories that can live only within four walls? And that I'll never again see the light of day? You take me for a fool? Don't you know who I am? Don't you realize that the grave is open at my feet? In a month I'll be up before the judges. In a month they'll decide I've got to get the axe. The axe, gentlemen! I'm no longer alive! I'm all alone now! All alone! Alone. Solo. I can die quiet. I've stopped beaming. I'm frozen.

MAURICE:

I'm with you.

GREEN EYES:

Frozen! You can get down on your knees before Snowball. You're right. The Number One Big Shot is Snowball. The Big Shot! Go kiss his toes, go on. He's got the luck to be a savage. He's got a right to kill people and even eat them. He lives in the jungle. That's his advantage over me. He's got his pet panthers. I'm alone, all alone. And too white. Too wilted by the cell. Too pale. Too wilted. But if you'd seen me before, with my hands in my pockets, and with my flowers, always with a flower in my teeth! They used to call me . . . Would you like to know? It was a nice nickname: Paulo with the Flowery Teeth! And now? I'm all alone. And my girl's dropping me. [To MAURICE] Would you have liked my girl?

MAURICE:

She did give me a sort of jolt. I admit it. Just seeing her through you drives me nearly crazy.

GREEN EYES [*bitterly*]:

I make a nice couple, eh? Does it get you excited?

MAURICE:

That's not what I mean. Though she doesn't have your mug, I see her all the same. You'll have a hard time shaking her off. That's why you've got to get revenge. Show me her picture.

GREEN EYES:

You see it every morning what I wash.

MAURICE:

Show it to me again. One last time.

GREEN EYES [*he opens his shirt brutally and reveals his torso to* MAURICE. *On it is tattooed a woman's face*]:

You like her?

MAURICE:

She's a beauty! Too bad I can't spit in her face. And that, what's that? [*He points to a spot on* GREEN EYES' *chest*] That your girl too?

GREEN EYES:

Drop it. Forget about her.

MAURICE:

I'd like to meet her. . . .

GREEN EYES:

You heard what I said: I want quiet. And fast. You're already enjoying what's happening to me. It's probably joy that's setting you both against her and against me. You're glad you're the only ones who can look at her.

MAURICE:

Don't get sore. It's because we're pals that I'm talking to you about her.

GREEN EYES:

I realize it. All too well. Make yourself scarce.

MAURICE:

You're not sore at me, are you? I'm capable of going and killing her, you know.

LEFRANC:

I'd like to see your face when blood starts flowing. You've got to have some in your veins first.

MAURICE:

What's needed is class! It's got to be written on your face. My face. . . .

LEFRANC:

If only you could see it! You and Green Eyes are a pair.

MAURICE:

Oh, Georgie, don't say that, I'm going to faint. You won't deny that I'm the best-looking kid in the prison. Take a squint at the little male!

[*He makes the gesture, already indicated, of tossing back a lock of hair*]

126

LEFRANC:

You louse!

MAURICE:

With a mug like mine, I can do anything I like. Even when I'm innocent, people think I'm guilty. I'm good-looking. It's faces like mine that some people would like to cut out of the newspapers. Eh, Georgie, for your collection? The gals would go nuts about it. Blood would flow. And tears. All the kids would feel like playing around with knives. It would be a holiday. They'd be dancing in the streets. A carnival for murderers.

LEFRANC:

You louse!

MAURICE:

Afterwards, the only thing left for me to do would be to turn into a rose and be plucked! But you, you'll never be in that class. Anyone can see that just from looking at you. You're not meant for that kind of thing. I'm not saying you're innocent, and I'm not saying that as a crook you're bust, but when it comes to crime, that's another matter.

LEFRANC:

What do you know about it?

MAURICE:

I know everything. I've been accepted by all the men, the real ones. I'm still young, but I've won their friendship. That's something you'll never do, never. You're not our kind. You'll never be. Even if you bumped a man off. No, we fascinate you.

LEFRANC:

It's Green Eyes who fascinates you! You're obsessed by him!

MAURICE:

That's a lie! Maybe I don't help him the way I'd like to help him, but you, you'd like him to help you.

LEFRANC:

Help me what?

MAURICE:

What? You want me to tell you? Remember the look on your face when the guard found all the photos of murderers in your mattress. What were you doing with them? What use were they to you? You had them all! All of them! Photos of Soklay, of Weidmann, of Vaché, of Angel Sun and God knows who else. I don't know them by heart. What were you doing with them? Were you saying mass to them? Were you praying to them? Eh, Georgie? At night, in your mattress, what were you doing, embalming them?

GREEN EYES:

Stop arguing. If you really want to bump off my girl, draw lots.

LEFRANC and MAURICE [*together*]:

Why? There's no need.

GREEN EYES:

Draw lots. I'm still boss. The lots will pick the instruments, but I'll be at the controls.

LEFRANC:

You're joking, Green Eyes.

GREEN EYES:

Do I look it? Where do you think you are? But pay close attention to what happens. Be on the look-out. You've made up your minds. You've made up your minds to bump off my girl. You've got to act fast. You've got to hurry up and choose so that you drop the subject. So that you stop talking about it until the one who's picked gets out of jail. Are you ready? Be careful. The axe is going to fall. One of you is going to get it in the neck. [*He places his fist on* MAURICE's *shoulder*] Will it be you? Are we going to make a little killer of you?

MAURICE:

You're not sore at me any more?

GREEN EYES:

Listen to me. We're droopy already because there's not enough air. Don't make me exert myself. I'll explain to both of you. Like a father. I'm saying that you've got to stay wide awake, because moments like that are awful. They're awful beacuse they're sweet. You follow me? They're too sweet.

LEFRANC:

What's too sweet?

GREEN EYES [*his voice getting more and more solemn*]:
It's by its sweetness that you recognize catastrophe. Me, I'm
no longer on the brink. I'm falling. I no longer risk anything,
as I've said. And Green Eyes is going to make you laugh:
I'm falling so sweetly, the thing that's making me fall is so
nice, that out of politeness I don't dare rebel. The day of the
crime . . . are you listening? The day of the crime, it was the
same. Are you listening? This concerns you, gentlemen. I
say "the day of the crime" and I'm not ashamed! Who is
there in the prison, on all the floors, who puts himself in my
class? Who that's as young as me, as good-looking as me,
has had the kind of misfortune that *I've* had? I say "the day
of the crime"! That day, more and more until . . .

LEFRANC [*gently*]:
. . . until the last gasp.

GREEN EYES:
Everything became more and more polite to me. In fact, a
man in the street raised his hat to me.

MAURICE:
Green Eyes, take it easy.

LEFRANC [*to* GREEN EYES]:
Go on. Continue.

MAURICE:
No. Stop. He's getting worked up by what you're saying.
He's all excited. [*To* LEFRANC] Yes, you're all excited. You
lap up other people's troubles.

GREEN EYES:
Keep quiet. I'm explaining. He took off his hat. That started
it. Then everything . . .

LEFRANC [*implacably*]:
Be specific.

GREEN EYES:
. . . everything began to move. There was nothing more to
be done. And that was why I had to kill someone. It's your
turn. You're going to bump off my girl. But be careful. I've
prepared everything for you. I'm giving you your chance.
I'll be leaving for the world of straw-hats and palm trees.
It's easy to begin a new life, you'll see. I realized it the
moment I killed the girl. I saw the danger. You understand
me? The danger of finding myself in someone else's boots.
And I was scared. I wanted to back up. Stop! No go! I tried
hard. I ran in all directions. I shifted. I tried every form and
shape so as not to be a murderer. Tried to be a dog, a cat, a
horse, a tiger, a table, a stone! I even tried, me too, to be a
rose! Don't laugh. I did what I could. I squirmed and
twisted. People thought I had convulsions. I wanted to turn
back the clock, to undo what I'd done, to live my life over
until before the crime. It looks easy to go backwards—but
my body couldn't do it. I tried again. Impossible. The people
around me kidded me. They didn't suspect the danger, until
the day they started getting anxious. My dance! You should
have seen my dance! I danced, boys, I danced!
[*Here the actor will have to invent a kind of dance which*

shows GREEN EYES *trying to go backwards in time. He contorts himself silently. He tries a spiral dance, on his own axis. His face expresses great suffering.* MAURICE *and* LEFRANC *watch him attentively*]

GREEN EYES [*dancing*]:
And I danced! Dance with me, Maurice.
[*He takes him by the waist and dances a few steps with him, but then thrusts him aside*]
Get the hell away! You hop as if you were`in a dance-hall!
[*He goes into his spiral dance again. Finally, he gets winded and stands still*]
And I danced! Then they searched. They suspected me. Afterwards, things happened by themselves. I simply made the gestures that led me as quietly as can be to the guillotine. Now I'm calm. And it's my job to organize your opportunity. You're going to draw lots. [*To* LEFRANC] Are you scared?

LEFRANC:
Let me alone.

GREEN EYES:
You'll get used to it. You've got to take the idea in easy stages. At the beginning, I scared myself. Now I like myself! Don't you like me?

LEFRANC:
Let me alone.

MAURICE [*to* GREEN EYES]:
You're flustering him. He's a leaf.

132

GREEN EYES:

Let yourselves drift. Just let yourself drift, Georgie. You'll always find someone to lend a helping hand. Maybe Snowball, if I'm no longer here.

LEFRANC:

Let me alone.

GREEN EYES:

You backing out? You don't have the style that Maurice has. I might have liked it to be you.

MAURICE [*banteringly*]:

Murderer.

GREEN EYES:

You've got to draw. You've got to draw lots.

MAURICE:

And . . . how . . . with what . . . you, how did you do it?

GREEN EYES:

That was different. It was destiny that took the form of my hands. It would be only fair to cut *them* off instead of my head. And for me everything became simpler. The girl was already under me. All I had to do was put one hand delicately on her mouth and the other delicately on her neck. It was over. But you . . .

MAURICE:

Give me advice.

LEFRANC:

You louse!

MAURICE:

Give me advice. Be specific. When it was finished, what did you do?

GREEN EYES:

Well, I told you. It all happened differently. First, I took the girl to my room. No one saw her going up. She wanted my lilacs.

MAURICE:

What?

GREEN EYES:

I had some lilacs between my teeth. The girl followed me. She was magnetized . . . I'm telling you everything, but let it guide you. Then . . . then she wanted to scream because I was hurting her. I choked her. I thought that once she was dead I'd be able to bring her back to life.

MAURICE:

And then what?

GREEN EYES:

Then? Well! *There* was the door!
[*He points to the right side of the cell and touches the wall*]
Impossible to get the body out. It took up too much room. And it was soft. First, I went to the window, in order to look outside. I didn't dare leave. I thought I saw a terrific crowd in the street. I thought they were waiting for me to show myself at the window. I moved the curtains aside a little . . .
[MAURICE *makes a gesture*] What?

MAURICE:

The lilacs? Did you leave them in her hair?

GREEN EYES [*sadly*]:
It's now that you warn me.

MAURICE:
Oh, Green Eyes, I didn't know. I'd have wanted to save
you. I swear. I'd have wanted to be there, I'd have wanted
to help you. . . .

GREEN EYES:
Keep still. You forget that I was observing you. You've had
a crush on her ever since the first day, since the morning
you saw me bare-chested in the shower. I realized it when
we got back. All your playing up to me was for her. Am
I wrong? When you looked at me, it was just to find out
how she was built and to imagine how our bodies fitted
together. And because I can't read or write you take me for
a cripple! But I've got eyes! Am I wrong?
[MAURICE *pulls a long face, like a child who has been
beaten*]
Speak up, I'm not a bully. Am I wrong? Don't try to kid
me. You destroyed me. You were in cahoots with God.
Lilacs! A whole little bunch in her hair, and no one to
warn me. And now? What am I to do? [*He looks at*
LEFRANC] Eh? What am I to do?

MAURICE [*to* GREEN EYES]:
Don't ask him anything. Don't ask him anything any more.
Can't you see the silly look on his puss? He's lapping you
up. He's gulping you down.

135

GREEN EYES:

Tell me what I'm to do?

MAURICE:

Just look at that puss of his. He's happy. Everything you say to him sinks right into his skin. You enter him through his skin and you don't know how you're going to get out. Let him alone.

LEFRANC:

I bother you.

MAURICE: [*to* LEFRANC]:

You want to get him down. You want to weaken him.

GREEN EYES [*sadly*]:

Listen, I tell you it's so sad that I wish it were night so I could try to cling to my heart. I'd like—I'm not ashamed to say it—I'd like, I'd like, I'd like, I'd like to . . . to cuddle up in my arms.

MAURICE:

Calm down, control yourself.

GREEN EYES [*still sadly*]:

And now you think I'm washed up. Green Eyes is completely gone to pot. You can get a close-up view of the big desperado. Touch me, you can touch me. [*Suddenly violent*] But don't be too sure! It may not take much to make me bounce back and lay you out flat! Better be on guard, all the same. You've just learned something about me that the police were never able to learn. You've just seen what I'm really like inside. But look out! I may never forgive you. You've had nerve enough to take me apart, but don't think I'm going to remain there in pieces. Green Eyes'll pull himself together. Green Eyes is already getting reorganized. I'm building myself up again. I'm healing. I'm making myself over. I'm getting stronger, more solid than a fortress. Stronger than the prison. You hear me, I *am* the prison! In my cells I guard big bruisers, brawlers, soldiers, plunderers! Be careful! I'm not sure that my guards and dogs can keep them back if I loose them on you! I've got ropes, knives, ladders! Be careful! There are sentinels on my rounds. There are spies everywhere. I'm the prison and I'm alone in the world.

MAURICE:
Calm yourself, Green Eyes.

GREEN EYES:
I'm preparing executions. I'm freeing convicts. Look out, boys! [*The door of the cell opens without anyone's appearing*] It's for me? Is it? She's here. [*He hesitates*] Is she here? Well, go tell her to go away.
[THE GUARD *enters*]

THE GUARD:
Hurry up. Your girl's waiting for you in the visitors' room.

GREEN EYES:
I'm not going.

THE GUARD:
What?

GREEN EYES:
I say I'm not going. You can tell her to go back home.

THE GUARD:
You mean it?

GREEN EYES:
Every word of it. It's over. The lady's dead.

THE GUARD:
Well, that's your affair. I'll give her the message. [*He looks about the cell*] Everything in order here?

LEFRANC:
Everything's in order, you can see for yourself.

THE GUARD [*to* LEFRANC]:
Is that so? What about that? [*He points to the unmade bed*] Answer. [*Silence*] You won't answer? I'm asking you why the bed's not made .
[*A long silence*]

GREEN EYES [*to* MAURICE *and* LEFRANC]:
Well, you guys? You know nothing about it. Speak up if it's you. Be frank. The boss won't make trouble.

LEFRANC:
We know no more about it than you.

THE GUARD [*still smiling*]:
I'd like to believe it. Frankness makes you choke. [*To* LEFRANC] When do you get out?

LEFRANC:
Day after tomorrow.

THE GUARD:
Good riddance.

LEFRANC [*aggressively*]:
Do I bother you? You should have said so yesterday. I'd have left this morning.

THE GUARD:
You'll change your tone with me. Otherwise, I'll let you have another taste of the guardroom.

LEFRANC:
I don't owe you any explanations. And\I don't owe any to this gentleman either. [*He points to* GREEN EYES] Nobody questions *you*.

THE GUARD:
Take it easy. [*He turns to* GREEN EYES *and* MAURICE] You see what happens when you want to be nice? Can't be done with guys like that. You end up by becoming inhuman. And then they claim that guards are brutes. [*To* LEFRANC] If you weren't so thick, you'd have realized I was doing my job. No one can say I pick on you. You may think you're smart, but I'm way ahead of you.

LEFRANC:
That remains to be proved.

THE GUARD:
It *is* proved. You don't know what a prison-guard has to see and put up with. You don't realize that he's got to be the very opposite of the thugs. I mean just that: the very oppo-

site. And he's also got to be the opposite of their friend. I'm not saying their enemy. Think about it. [*He reaches into his pocket and takes out some cigarettes which he hands to* GREEN EYES] Here, this is proof. [*To* GREEN EYES] There, Green Eyes. They're from your pal. Snowball sends you two cigarettes.

GREEN EYES:
O.K. [*He puts a cigarette into his mouth and hands the other to* MAURICE]

MAURICE:
Don't bother.

GREEN EYES:
Don't you want it?

MAURICE:
No.

THE GUARD:
He's right. Too young to smoke. The black boy asked me to tell you that you mustn't worry. That guy's a real pal of yours. [*Embarrassed silence*] Well, what about your girl?

GREEN EYES:
I've told you. It's over.

THE GUARD:
Still, she seemed to like those green eyes of yours. I was watching her just before. She's a good-looking girl. Nice figure.

140

GREEN EYES [*smiling*]:

You won't be seeing her again when she leaves here, will you?

THE GUARD [*also smiling*]:

Would that bother you?

GREEN EYES:

Oh, after all, if you like her, try your luck.

THE GUARD:

No kidding? You mean I can?

GREEN EYES:

Why not? I've left the earth. Life tires me. And besides, you're not like the other guards.

THE GUARD:

Son of a gun! So really mean it? You're leaving her right in the palm of my hand?

GREEN EYES:

She's all yours [*They shake hands*]

THE GUARD:

Now I understand. When she looked you up and down behind the grating, she wanted to give herself a last treat.

GREEN EYES:

It was last Thursday she said good-bye to me. You're right. with those baby-doll eyes of hers she was giving me the air.

THE GUARD:

Do you think she'll lose by the exchange?

GREEN EYES:

You'll talk to her about me. You'll take my place. I'm counting on you to replace me when my head's cut off.

THE GUARD:

O.K. We'll adopt you. And if you want anything from the kitchen, let me know. You can have whatever you want. [*To* LEFRANC] You still don't realize what a guard is. In order to know [*he points to* GREEN EYES] you've got to be in his boots.

LEFRANC:

That doesn't change the fact that he'd have liked Maurice and me to get all the blame and be sent to the guardroom. Because naturally he's the Man!

GREEN EYES:

You bellyaching? For so little.

LEFRANC:

To you it's very little. [*To* MAURICE] You saw how 'he accused us. . . .

MAURICE:

Green Eyes? He wasn't accusing anyone. He decided why the bed was unmade .

LEFRANC:

And I was the one who got it.

GREEN EYES:

Come off it, will you? What did I say? The truth. I said it in front of the boss because he's a decent guy. There's no risk with him. He's way ahead of lots of the convicts.

LEFRANC:

A guard's a guard. [*He puts on the jacket that* GREEN EYES *has just tossed on the bed*]

GREEN EYES:

He's different.

LEFRANC:

It's no doubt because of you that the cell is under his protection. Because of the man. The tattooed man.

GREEN EYES:

You're the one who's trying to act like a man. You're trying to strut. A man doesn't have to strut. He knows he's a man and that's all that matters.

LEFRANC [*to* MAURICE]:

You hear that?

MAURICE [*curtly*]:

Green Eyes is right.

LEFRANC:

To you, anything Green Eyes says and does is perfectly natural. You'd be willing to be cut in two if you could take his place. It's perfectly natural. Just because it's Green Eyes.

MAURICE:

That's *my* business.

LEFRANC:

Only don't get any false ideas into your head. His friends, the real ones, are on the floor above. You were wasting your time defending him the way you did just before. Green Eyes gets his orders from the other world. They send him cigarettes—from where? From the other side of the water. Brought by a special guard, in full uniform, who offers him friendship on a platter. A message from the heart. You were talking about Snowball's smile weren't you? And you thought it was meant for me, didn't you? You were wrong. The gentleman has already plucked it from Snowball's teeth. All the prisoners are divided into two warring camps, and the two kings smile at each other above our heads—or behind our backs—or even before our very eyes. And at the end they make a present of their girls. . . .

GREEN EYES:

That'll do, Georgie. My girl is at *my* disposal.

LEFRANC:

You've got all the rights, you're the man. What you've done entitles you to everything. All Big Shot has to do is whistle and we start circling round and round the cell. . . .

THE GUARD:

Come on, stop arguing. I'm going over to see Snowball. *He's* always singing. So long.

[*He leaves*]

GREEN EYES [*to* LEFRANC]:

Yes Sir! You're right. If I felt like it, I'd make you circle round and round like the horses in a merry-go-round. The way I used to waltz the girls around. You think I can't? I do what I like here. I'm the man here, yes Sir! I can go walking in the halls, up and down the stairs, I can go across the court and the yards. I'm the one they respect. They're afraid of me. Maybe I'm not as strong as Snowball because his crime was a little more necessary than mine. Because he killed in order to rob and loot, but, like him, I killed in order to live, and now I'm smiling. I've understood my crime. I've understood everything and I'm brave enough to be all alone. In broad daylight.

LEFRANC:

Don't get excited, Green Eyes. I've understood too. And I admit you're entitled to everything. I did all I could so that the letters to your girl were as nice as possible. You've got a right to be sore at me. I was taking your place.

GREEN EYES:

I'm not sore at you. I don't give a damn. The letters were nice. They were too nice. Maybe you thought you were writing to your own girl. . . .

LEFRANC:

No, never. I wrote nice letters because I put myself completely in your place. I got into your skin.

GREEN EYES:

But in order to get into my skin, you've got to be my size. And to be my size, you've got to do as I do. Don't deny it. You'd like to be chummy with the guards. You'd like that. But you're not strong enough. Maybe some day you'll know what a guard is. But you'll have to pay the price.

LEFRANC:

I wanted to separate you from your girl, Green Eyes. I did

all I could. I did what I could to isolate you from the world and to separate the cell, and even the prison, from the world. And I think I've succeeded. I wanted the whole world to know that we're here and that we're peaceful here. Among ourselves. I don't want a single breath of air to come from outside. And I'm working at it. More than anyone else. I wanted us to be brothers. That's why I mixed up the clothes. You remember? I repeat, I've been working for the prison.

GREEN EYES:
The prison is mine, and I'm running the show here.

MAURICE:
And it's a sell-out.

GREEN EYES:
What was that you said?

MAURICE:
Nothing.

GREEN EYES:
I sell out? So what? You wouldn't dare aks me to be on the up and up, would you? It would be inhuman to expect that of a man who'll be dead in two months. What does that mean, being on the up and up, after what I've done? After taking the big leap into the void, after cutting myself off from human beings as I've done, you still expect me to respect your rules? I'm stronger than you and I can do as I like.

LEFRANC:

I understand you. And I also understand what he calls your
double-crossing. I like you that way. Keep lowering yourself.

MAURICE:

Green Eyes. . . .

GREEN EYES:

I'm listening to your charges.

MAURICE:

I didn't say anything.

GREEN EYES:

Well?

MAURICE:

Nothing. I think you've been double-crossing. I realize
now that you've always been double-crossing! I've got a right
to tell you so because it hurt me just now to discover that
you were the black boy's friend. And you didn't let us know.

GREEN EYES:

And what if I like to double-cross? Who are you, Georgie
and you? A pair of small-time crooks. It's not the likes of you
who can judge me. I look for friends in the prison and I've
got a right to. Snowball is at my side. He encourages me.
If we get out of it, we'll go to Cayenne together, and
if I get the axe, I know he'll follow me. But what am I
to you? You think I haven't guessed? Here in the cell I'm
the one who bears the brunt. The brunt of what—I don't
know. I'm illiterate. But I know I need a strong back. Like
Snowball. He bears the same weight. But for the whole

prison. Maybe there's someone else, a Number One Big Shot, who bears it for the whole world! You can laugh in my face, I've got rights. I'm the man.

MAURICE:

To me, you're still Green Eyes. A terrific guy. But you've lost your force, your fine criminal force. You belong to your girl more than you realize.

GREEN EYES:

You're wrong.

MAURICE:

When I was in cell 108 and used to pass in front of your door on my way through the hall, all I could see was your hand that put the bowl through the cage. I saw the ring on your fourth finger. I was sure you were a complete man because of your ring, but I didn't think that you really had a girl. Now you have one. But I forgive you everything because I saw how you broke down before.

GREEN EYES:

You make me laugh. Shut up and go argue with Georgie.

MAURICE:

That's another thing that turns my stomach. If I'm no longer with you, I'll have to be with him. [*He turns to* LEFRANC] You nauseate me, yes, you nauseate me. I've got to watch out for you. You're capable of getting up at night and strangling me.

LEFRANC:

I don't need the night for that.

MAURICE:

You nauseate me. It's you who heckle Green Eyes. It's you who destroyed our friendship. You were jealous of him. You're furious because you haven't done anything as grand as he. You wanted to put yourself in his class.

LEFRANC:

You, you small-time crook, what wouldn't you do to put yourself in his class?

MAURICE:

That's a lie! I'll help him. And I'll keep helping him. Don't think you can make friends with me just because I'm feeling low. I may be a coward, Lefranc, but I'm warning you, I'll defend his crime. . . .

LEFRANC:

Did you hear his crime? And you saw him, the murderer, practically in tears!

MAURICE:

You've got no right to talk like that, Georgie! You hear me? No right to laugh! It's because I saw him in that state that my friendship is so deep. I pity him now. I pity the finest murderer in the world. And it's fine to pity so great a monument that's crumbling. It's because I saw him so broken, and almost on account of me, that I felt pity. Whereas you . . .

LEFRANC:

Me?

149

MAURICE:
Listening to him excited you.

LEFRANC:
Well, that was part of my program too. And I'm the one who succeeds. Green Eyes did what he had to . . .

MAURICE:
And you? You? What have you done that's better? What have you to boast about? The marks on your wrists maybe? The galley? Your burglaries? You don't need any talent for that.

LEFRANC:
I'd have liked to see you with Serge during that job on River Street. In the dark with people shooting at us from windows. . . .

MAURICE [*ironically*]:
Serge? Serge who? Probably Serge de Lenz!

LEFRANC:
Serge de Lenz in person. It was with him that I got my start. You don't believe me?

MAURICE:
You've got to prove it. Because the cells are full of the most terrific stories imaginable. There are times when it all hangs in the air, and the air gets so thick you feel like puking. And the worst of all are the ones they invent to make themslves look big. Racketeering, trafficking in gold, pearls, diamonds! It reeks. Phony dollars, cash-boxes, furs! And galley-slaves!

LEFRANC:
Go to hell!

MAURICE:
  The galley!

LEFRANC:
  You threatening me?

  [*He goes for* MAURICE *and tries to seize him.* GREEN EYES
  separates them brutally]

GREEN EYES:
  It's not time for that yet. You're a pair of lunatics. I'll
  lay you both out on the cement.

  [*In struggling,* MAURICE *tears* LEFRANC'*s shirt*]

MAURICE:
  It's him! It's always him!

GREEN EYES [*staring at* LEFRANC'*s chest*]:
  But . . . you're tattooed!

MAURICE [*examing the mark*]:
  "The Avenger"! Terrific.

LEFRANC:
  Let me alone.

GREEN EYES:
  "The Avenger"? I served on her before I was sent to the
  naval prison at Calvi. A fast little submarine. Were you a
  sailor, Georgie?

LEFRANC:
  Let me alone.

GREEN EYES:
  Were you?

LEFRANC:
  I've never been in the navy.

MAURICE:
Well, Avenger?

GREEN EYES:
When I was in jail, in Clairvaux, I knew a guy called the
Avenger. A bruiser. And I've known others, men as well
as boats. There was the Panther, port of Brest.

LEFRANC:
Poissy Penitentiary.

GREEN EYES:
The Slasher, Riom Penitentiary.

LEFRANC:
Port of Cherboug.

GREEN EYES:
The Cyclone, Fontevrault Jail.

LEFRANC:
Port of Brest.

GREEN EYES:
How come you know them if you've never been anywhere?

LEFRANC:
Everyone knows about them. They're things that have out-
grown what they are. I've known all the real signs of bad
luck for a long time.

MAURICE:
You don't know much if all you know is the signs.

GREEN EYES:
What about the Avalanche?

LEFRANC:
Toulon.

GREEN EYES:

The Avalanche! Terrific thighs. He knifed three men. Twenty years of hard labor. He did them at Fort Hâ!

MAURICE:

He's talking about boats and you about yeggs at Cayenne.

LEFRANC:

We understand each other.

MAURICE:

I'd like to believe it. You've got a long way to go to be in Green Eyes' class.

GREEN EYES:

Avenger is a title. It's not an easy one to bear. There are three of them already. The Avenger at Clairvaux, with a dozen armed robberies. Got fifteen years. At Tréous, another Avenger. Tried to murder a cop. But the most terrible of all is Robert Garcia, known as Robert the Avenger, at the pen in Fréjus. He's the champ you've got to beat. And to do that you need a murder with all the trimmings. Nothing else'll do.

LEFRANC:

Green Eyes . . .

GREEN EYES [smiling]:

I'm here, don't worry. Don't lose your bearings. I'm at the wheel. Now you understand that I needed Snowball's friendship. He's the one who's holding us up. And don't worry. He's solid. He's squarely planted in crime. Steady

153

on his feet. You were right. The whole prison's under his authority, but right under him is me . . . And . . . you too, you'll be entitled to my girl.

MAURICE [*going up to* LEFRANC]:
Wait, hold it, the gentleman's not tattooed. It's only drawn in ink.

LEFRANC:
You louse!

MAURICE:
"Avenger"! He got it from a book, like the story of the galley.

LEFRANC:
I told you to shut up or I'll bash your head in!

MAURICE:
Because Green Eyes talks to you, because he listens to you, you bask in his glory. Only, *his* tattoos aren't phony. He wasn't scared of being stuck by needles.

LEFRANC [*threateningly*]:
Shut it!

MAURICE [*to* GREEN EYES]:
He's repulsive. What about your girl, you going to let him have your girl!

GREEN EYES [*smiling*]:
Did *you* want her?

MAURICE:
Your girl! Who's engraved in your skin! Oh, Green Eyes!— Where did she come up to on you?

GREEN EYES [*he makes a gesture*]:
Here!

MAURICE:
Ah!

LEFRANC:
Don't be shy, go fondle one another.

MAURICE:
I'm talking about his girl. I've a right to.

LEFRANC:
If I grant it.

MAURICE:
To talk about his girl?

LEFRANC:
That's right, mister. And from now on resign yourself to reckoning with me.

MAURICE [*ironically*]:
All the same, I can't ask you questions about her. You're not planning to draw her on your skin like . . . [*he makes the gesture of tossing back an invisible lock of hair*] like "the Avenger"! If I'm concerned with his girl, it's because Green Eyes allows me to be.

LEFRANC:
A few minutes ago, you despised him.

MAURICE:
Never. It was you. You're the one who got a kick out of making him tell his story in full detail. You're a coward.

LEFRANC:
It was you who wormed it out of him. You gently drew the words. . . .

MAURICE:

That's a lie. I did what I could to make it easy for him. He knows it. I don't expect a man to do my work for me. I expect nothing. I'm ready for anything. When I slip up, I'll take what's coming to me. That's how I'm built. But you, you're in a fog. When you circle round, you watch us live. You watch us struggle and you're envious. The story of the liacs made you glow! Admit it! All we saw was your lousy mug leaning forward, with its dead eyes, circling round the cell. You're going to chew that business of the liacs over and over! It's already fattening you up.

LEFRANC:

It's beginning to work on me, you're right.

MAURICE:

Is it giving you strength? It's rising up. Is it rising up to your lips? Are the lilacs rising up to your teeth?

LEFRANC:

Right to my fingertips, Maurice. Shall I tell you what the story of the crime and the lilacs makes me feel? Not pity, but joy! You hear me? Joy! He's broken another thread that holds him to the world. He's cut off from the police. Soon he'll be cut off from his girl!

MAURICE:

You bastard! You're planning. . . .

LEFRANC:

My work, mine.

156

MAURICE:

And Green Eyes is the one who's got to suffer for it! He's
the one who paid for it. The one who's been chosen. And
if I attract trouble, it's not by guzzling other men's adven-
tures. It's because of my mug, as I've told you. I'm a marked
man, me too, but my real mark is my mug! My mug, my
cute little yegg's mug. I've made up my mind to defend
myself. You stink up the cell and I'm going to get rid of
your garbage. You nauseate us. You're a phony. Phony to
the marrow of your bones. Your story about the galley and
the marks on your wrists is phony, and your secrets
with our girl are phony, and all your complications about
Snowball are phony, and your tattoos are phony, and your
anger is phony, and . . .

LEFRANC:

Stop it!

MAURICE:

Your frankness is phony, your gab is phony . . .

LEFRANC:

Stop it or I'll smack.

MAURICE:

I'm going to strip you. I want to leave you naked. You feed
on others. You dress yourself up, you decorate yourself
with our jewels, I accuse you! You steal our crimes! You
wanted to know what a real crime's made of. I was watching
you take it apart.

LEFRANC:
Shut your mouth.

MAURICE:
I refuse to let you off, I'll continue. . . .

LEFRANC:
Stop it. Let me breathe.

MAURICE:
You're bloated with our life.
[*He makes the gesture of tossing back his lock of hair*]

LEFRANC:
Maurice. I'm telling you to stop. And stop tossing your head like a whore.

MAURICE:
Why? [*Laughing*] Is the gentleman afraid I'll disturb his bunch of lilacs?

LEFRANC:
I am. And now you're going for a ride with me. For a long, long ride, Get ready for me. Here I come. *I'm* the Avenger. No more curling up and sleeping under Green Eyes' wing.

MAURICE [*to* GREEN EYES]:
Big boy. . . .
[*Then, looking at* LEFRANC, *he again makes the gesture with his hand and head*]

LEFRANC:
It's too late. Don't scream.

[GREEN EYES *is perched on a basin and dominates the stage*

158

as LEFRANC, *smiling, bears down on* MAURICE *who, in the presence of this radiant smile, also smiles*]

GREEN EYES [*his face drawn*]:
You wear me down, both of you. You put a bigger strain on me than on yourselves. Get it over with and stop jabbering.

MAURICE [*frightened*]:
You're crazy, Georgie. I haven't done anything!

LEFRANC:
Don't scream, it's too late.
[*He blocks* MAURICE *in a corner and strangles him.* MAURICE *slides to the floor between* LEFRANC's *spread legs.* LEFRANC *straightens up*]

GREEN EYES [*in a changed voice, after a moment's silence*]:
What have you done? It's not true, Lefranc, you haven't killed him? [*He looks at the lifeless* MAURICE] That's a neat job. [LEFRANC *looks exhausted*] Neat enough to get you to Guiana.

LEFRANC:
What'll we do? Help me, Green Eyes.

GREEN EYES [*approaching the door*]:
You bastard! Me help you?

LEFRANC [*staggered*]:
Huh? But . . .

GREEN EYES:
You realize what you've just done? Rubbed out Maurice, who hadn't done anything. Killed him for nothing! For the glory of it!

LEFRANC:

Green Eyes . . . You're not going to let me down?

GREEN EYES:

Don't talk to me. Don't touch me. Do you know what misfortune is? Don't you know I kept hoping to avoid it? And you thought you could become, all by yourself, without the help of heaven, as great as me! Maybe overshadow me? You fool, don't you realize it's impossible to overshadow me? I didn't want anything—you hear me?—I didn't want what happened to me to happen. It was all given to me. A gift from God or the devil, but something I didn't want. And now, here we are with a corpse on our hands.

LEFRANC [at first overwhelmed, then pulling himself together]:

I realized. I realized I'd never be with you, Green Eyes. But I want you to know I'm stronger than anyone else. I won't have to dance to undo my crime, because I willed it.

GREEN EYES:

That's the danger. To blow in casually and bump off a kid! Why . . . I don't even have the heart to mention the name for that sort of criminal . . . I never knew I was strangling the girl. I was carried away. I didn't want to catch up with anyone. I risked everything. I made a false move and fell flat on my face.

LEFRANC:

I want to be let alone. I want everyone to let me alone! I wanted to become what you were. . . .

160

GREEN EYES:

What we are in spite of ourselves. And what I wanted to destroy by dancing.

LEFRANC:

But what you're proud of having become. You're radiant. You . . . you're beginning to be radiant. I wanted to take your place . . . your luminous place. . . .

GREEN EYES:

And what about our crimes?

LEFRANC:

Including the crimes.

GREEN EYES:

Not ours.

LEFRANC:

I did what I could, out of a yearning for misfortune.

GREEN EYES:

You don't know the first thing about misfortune if you think you can choose it. I didn't want mine. It chose me. It fell on my shoulders and clung to me. I tried everything to shake it off. I struggled, I boxed, I danced, I even sang, and, odd as it may seem, I refused it at first. It was only when I saw that everything was irremediable that I quieted down. I've only just accepted it. It had to be total.

LEFRANC:

It's thanks to me. . . .

GREEN EYES:

I don't give a damn! It's only now that I'm really settling down in misfortune and making it my heaven. And you, you try to get there by fraud. . . .

LEFRANC:

I'm stronger than you. My misfortune comes from something deeper. It comes from myself.

GREEN EYES:

I don't give a damn! And I refuse to argue.

[*He knocks at the door*]

LEFRANC:

What are you doing?

GREEN EYES:

I'm calling the guards. [*He raps at the door*] You'll know by the look on their mugs whether you can be with us or not.

LEFRANC:

Green Eyes!

GREEN EYES:

You bastard!

LEFRANC:

I really am all alone!

[*Sound of a key. The door opens.* THE GUARD *appears, smiling. He leers at* GREEN EYES]

CURTAIN